Hand-Built Outdoor Furniture

Hand-Built
OUTDOOR
FURNITURE

20 STEP-BY-STEP PROJECTS
Anyone Can Build

KATIE JACKSON

with photos by
ELLEN BLACKMAR

TIMBER PRESS
PORTLAND, OREGON

Photo credits appear on page 259.

Published in 2016 by Timber Press

The Haseltine Building
133 S.W. Second Avenue, Suite 450
Portland, Oregon 97204-3527
timberpress.com

Printed in China
Cover and book design by Skye McNeill

Library of Congress Cataloging-in-Publication Data

Names: Jackson, Katie, 1985- author. | Blackmar, Ellen.
Title: Hand-built outdoor furniture: 20 step-by-step projects anyone can
    build / Katie Jackson with photographs by Ellen Blackmar.
Description: Portland, Oregon: Timber Press, 2016. | Includes index.
Identifiers: LCCN 2015036652 | ISBN 9781604695830
Subjects: LCSH: Outdoor furniture—Design and construction. | Furniture
    making—Amateurs' manuals.
Classification: LCC TT197.5.O9 J33 2016 | DDC 684.1—dc23 LC
    record available at http://lccn.loc.gov/2015036652

A catalog record for this book is also available from the British Library.

To everyone who's ever said, "I could never do that!"

Contents

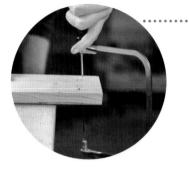

Part Two

PROJECTS

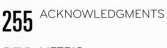

PREFACE

Be confident!

With a few basic tools and a weekend, you can build a beautiful piece of furniture out of wood for your outdoor space. In my experience, woodworking is mostly about problem solving. How can I make this more structurally stable? How should I correct this mistake? Everyone solves problems differently, and over the course of my woodworking career building furniture alongside other builders and teaching young woodworkers, I've enjoyed seeing a multitude of ways to cut a board or calculate a measurement.

In my woodworking classes, I provide an example of a project I've built, such as the flower box on page 76—a student favorite—and ask the students to figure out their own process to build it. The projects I provide have no specific measurements and no written instructions, but once they study the pieces, the students can easily see how they are constructed and re-create the projects with their own desired measurements and personal flourishes. My students often use interesting and innovative ways to get to the same end point. I learn a lot from them, and I often notice a trend: once given a basic understanding of how to use woodworking tools and machines, many of the younger students are thrilled to be given the chance to solve problems through their own creativity, while many of the older students, especially adults, request help every step of the way and keep asking what to do next.

Nonetheless, the intrepid younger students and the cautious older students, when given the same instruction on tool use and the same amount of time, all seem to produce the same caliber of high-quality woodworking. Perhaps this is because as we get older, we become more critical of ourselves. We may expect ourselves to be skilled in subjects we've never studied. We may be worried someone will see our work and criticize it, or that our work is not as good as someone else's. That kind of worry can prevent us from ever starting or continuing to learn a new skill.

I encourage you to just begin. Getting away from glowing screens and doing something with your hands is a satisfying use of spare time. Even if your project ends up looking different from what you expected, you'll have exercised your brain and body to create something all your own. We are all our own worst critic, but remember, your friends and family won't see the dent in the board from dropping it on the floor; they'll see a beautiful new piece of furniture that you made with your own hands. Take pride in your work, continue to be willing to learn new skills, and share your newfound skills with others. You're continuing an ancient human tradition.

Part One

BUILDING YOUR OWN
GARDEN FURNITURE

Making furniture for the outdoors is a great way to learn woodworking and problem-solving skills. It's a low-pressure hobby, because you don't have to match a specific interior decor style, and anything you build yourself is going to be more special than its store-bought equivalent. Adding hand-built pieces to your garden, yard, porch, or balcony will make the space uniquely yours and will lend a place for your eye or your body to rest.

With just a few tools, you can turn your garage, basement, or shed into a workshop. If you do not have enough space or cannot purchase tools, look into local woodworking clubs, makerspaces, shared workshop spaces, or community centers with wood shops. I built all the projects in this book at a local hackerspace that has a wood shop. Shared workshops not only have the tools and machines that you'll need, they also have the benefit of a built-in community of people who like to learn from one another and collaborate.

Part One of this book demonstrates the basics of using woodworking tools and machines, and it covers several fundamental construction techniques. Part Two presents step-by-step instructions and photographs for twenty outdoor furniture projects. All the materials used to make the projects can be found at local hardware and lumber stores as well as big-box home-improvement chains. You'll only need basic tools—no table saws or routers. A miter saw and a cordless drill/driver will become your best friends.

The projects in this book increase in complexity. If you are a beginner, I suggest starting with the universally useful—and quick—Shaker pegboard shelf. Then make one or two other easy pieces and work your way up to whichever projects strike your fancy. The projects draw visual inspiration from a range of sources, from Shaker designs to cottage-style furniture to midcentury-modern icons, and all are designed for maximum visual appeal and sturdy construction with minimum effort. I attempted to include a range of designs to suit a variety of tastes, but any of these projects can be customized to your liking by changing details such as paint color, shapes, or measurements.

Almost every project uses a specific method of counterboring and plugging screw holes to join two pieces of wood. Please review and use this method, even if this is not what you have used before. You'll save yourself from hours of headaches from split wood and incorrectly driven screws, and your projects, with flush plugs covering up the screws, will look polished and sophisticated.

Shop Confidently for Lumber

When I was a teenager, I missed out on building many projects because I was too intimidated to go to a lumberyard alone. I was afraid someone would think I didn't know what I was doing and laugh at me. While it is true that I didn't know what I was doing, I didn't realize that the people who work at lumberyards are eager to help you find what you need—they're not there to laugh at teenage girls. When I overcame my fear and finally started shopping for lumber and materials, the vast majority of my experiences at lumberyards and hardware stores were with extremely friendly and helpful staff. If you need help, don't hesitate to ask. It is because of my own years of timidity that I give you guidelines for shopping in such detail; while this all may seem obvious to someone who's been doing it their whole life, it isn't second nature to others.

Before going to the store, make a list of all the lumber and materials you'll need. Measure the length of the inside of your car or truck. If you have a sedan, you'll have to put the lumber in through the trunk all the way up to the space between the two front seats. In my sedan, I can transport a 12-foot board if I fit it all the way from the top of the dashboard to the back of the trunk, but I generally like to stick with 10-foot and shorter lengths so I don't have to worry about the wood cracking my windshield. Most stores will be happy to cut lumber down to smaller sizes so you can fit it in your car. If the store is cutting the wood down to size, be sure there is at least an inch of extra space on either side of the cut so you can cut the wood to its proper length later.

At big-box hardware stores, there is usually an entrance specifically for contractors, but anyone can use this entrance and the registers near it—this is where the lumber is. Park in a space near the contractors' entrance (but don't park your car in the loading area).

At the store, locate the lumber you want and then pick up a lumber cart. Go through the piles of lumber to pick the best boards and neatly replace all the discarded boards when you're finished. If each board has a bar code, place them in the cart with all the bar codes at the same end—this helps the checkout clerk. After checking out, you can bring your car up to the contractors' entrance to load the boards, or bring your cart to your parking space. If you're by yourself and need to leave your cart in the store while you get your car, you can ask the checkout clerk where to put your cart while you get your car.

Board Basics

Throughout the book I refer to a board's different surfaces—its faces, edges, ends, and corners. The two faces of a board are its widest and longest parts. If a board is 1 inch × 4 inches × 6 feet, 1 inch indicates its thickness, 4 inches indicates its width, and 6 feet indicates its length.

The width of the edges is the thickness of the board, the "1" in a 1 inch × 4 inch. A 1 inch × 4 inch board is referred to as a 1 × 4 (pronounced *one by four*). The board's grain runs lengthwise along its two faces and two edges. The end of the grain is on the two ends of a board. The corners are all 90-degree angles—a board has twelve corners.

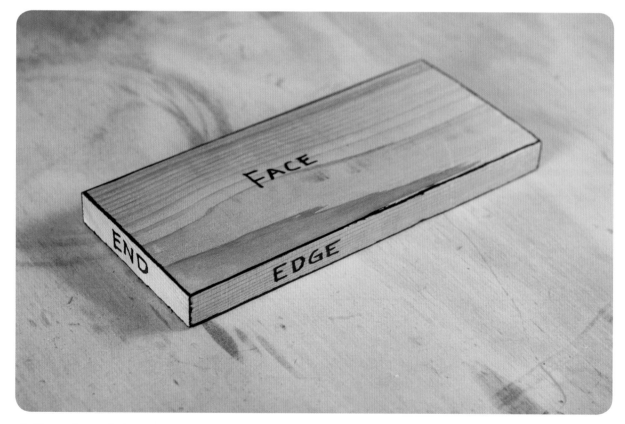

▲ The surfaces of a board consist of its faces, edges, and ends.

Choosing Boards

- At the hardware store, look for dimensional lumber—that is, lumber that is flat on all sides.

- Choose *common* boards, which are basic and inexpensive, or *select* boards, which have fewer knots and a straighter grain. These boards should already be planed flat on both faces.

- When you're choosing a board, turn it on its edge and look down its length as if you are checking a pool cue to see if it is straight.

- It's fine if a board has a few knots, but see if the wood around the knots is warped, twisted, or cupped. If it is, choose another board.

- Look for cracks and gouges in the wood. Like a run in a stocking, the cracks may begin to extend farther down the length of a board. If you won't need the entire length of a board, you can cut the end with the crack off.

- Buy untreated wood. Pressure-treated wood lasts longer outside, but contains chemicals that I don't want you or the living things in your yard to be exposed to. If the wood in your store is unlabeled, you can generally tell pressure-treated wood from untreated wood because it feels wetter than untreated wood and sometimes has a slight green tint. Two projects in this book use a few pieces of pressure-treated wood: the bistro table has legs that are pressure-treated and the torchiere's fence-post cap is pressure treated. Always wear a dust mask when working with pressure-treated wood.

Softwoods

Conifers, trees that have needles rather than leaves, produce a softer, more forgiving wood to work with. Lighter in weight than hardwoods, softwoods are easily sanded. Softwoods are also more pliable than hardwoods—if the last boards in a construction don't quite line up, you can push them into place with your hands before screwing them together.

Types of Softwood

For most of the projects in this book, I used pine, which is the most abundant, renewable, and affordable 1-inch-thick wood in my region, the northeastern United States. I also recommend cedar, which is a little more expensive, has a darker, richer color, is less heavy, and is resistant to rot and pests. Cedar smells absolutely delicious and lasts well outdoors. If you live in a region where sustainably harvested redwood is available, it's a great option—its pink, orange, and red-brown colors are irresistible, and it holds up nicely outdoors. The colors of cedar and redwood will deepen and mellow beautifully over the years when exposed to sunlight and air.

Lumber Measurements: Nominal versus actual

Before a softwood board is sold, it is milled down into a flat piece that has 90-degree angles. After it is milled down, a board nominally called a 2 × 4 will actually measure 1½ inches × 3½ inches. Similarly, a nominal 1 × 3 board will measure ¾ × 2½ inches.

Woodworking Materials: Use products suitable for outdoor furniture

GLUE Be sure to use weatherproof wood glue marked for exterior work. For projects like the ones in this book, buy glue in small bottles. I needed only one 8-ounce bottle of glue to make the entire list of projects in this book, and I still had some left over. If you buy a large bottle of glue and leave it for a while unused, it may harden.

SOFTWOOD SIZE CHART: NOMINAL DIMENSION VERSUS ACTUAL DIMENSION

Nominal Size	Actual Size
1 × 2	¾ × 1½
1 × 3	¾ × 2½
1 × 4	¾ × 3½
1 × 5	¾ × 4½
1 × 6	¾ × 5½
1 × 8	¾ × 7¼
1 × 10	¾ × 9¼
1 × 12	¾ × 11¼
2 × 2	1½ × 1½
2 × 4	1½ × 3½

FEET AND INCH EQUIVALENTS FOR STANDARD-SIZE BOARDS

Unlike a board's thickness and width, which is measured in inches, a board's length is measured in feet. And unlike nominal sizes for thickness and width, the length of single boards is usually actual (although it may be up to a half inch longer). For quick reference when you are calculating how many boards to buy of a certain size, following is a table showing feet-to-inch conversions for standard-size boards. Buy a few more inches than you'll need for your project to accommodate for the blade's width, or kerf, and to cut the ends at ninety degrees.

Feet	Inches
6	72
8	96
10	120
12	144

PAINT AND STAIN Use paint and stain labeled for use on exterior projects. See page 46 for more information.

SCREWS Choose deck screws. They will not rust. Most deck screws come in either a Phillips head (plus-sign shaped) or Robertson (square shaped), also known as a square drive. You can use either. Square drive bits usually come inside a box of square drive screws, and these bits can be inserted into a quick-flip drive. Most of the screw heads in these projects will be covered with plugs, so aesthetics shouldn't factor into which type of screw you use. See page 38 for more information.

Durability

Furniture designed for the outdoors won't last forever. Depending on how you finish, store, and care for your pieces, and, of course, depending on the climate where you live, your furniture might last from two years to a few decades outside. If you use good construction techniques, reapply paint or protective stain every year, and store your pieces in a dry place during winter, your pieces will last a long time. Part of the beauty of outdoor furniture is the way it seasons: the deepening of the color of the wood, the dents from getting hit by wayward Frisbees on a spring day, the chip from that time your cousin attempted a backflip off the tabletop, and the cracks from a deep snow settling on the slats on a still winter's night. You can bring your chaise longue inside every time it rains, or you can channel artist Andy Goldsworthy and appreciate the beauty of your furniture's aging and eventual decay.

Tools of the Trade

This section presents the machines and tools needed for basic woodworking. A few essential tools are all you'll need to make the projects in this book. You won't necessarily need every tool listed here, but you'll need tools to measure, cut, and drill.

Hand tools are powered by the woodworker, held in the woodworker's hands, and applied to stationary wood. Power tools, which can save you time and effort, are battery powered or plugged in to a power source. They are held in the woodworker's hands and used on stationary wood. Woodworking machines are stationary and connected to a power source. They are usually attached to a work surface or stand on their own on the floor and the woodworker applies the wood to the machine.

Measuring Tools

ADJUSTABLE SQUARE Also known as a combination square, an adjustable square is an indispensable tool for your collection. When the lock bolt (the knurled knob) is loosened, the head can be slid along the ruler and tightened to set a specific distance. An adjustable square set at a certain location can be used to make multiple marks all at the same exact distance, or slid along the edge of a board with a pencil at the end of a ruler to make a mark along a board's entire length.

FRAMING SQUARE Framing squares have two large blades that form a right angle. Use a framing square for large projects, like when you need to ensure a table leg is 90 degrees.

SPEED SQUARE When you need to mark an accurate 90-degree or 45-degree angle, use a speed square. Hook an edge of the speed square over the edge or end of a board and trace a line along the blade.

TAPE MEASURE Tape measures and squares are probably the most commonly used tools for measuring. A 16-foot tape measure is usually sufficient for woodworking projects.

Saws

BAND SAWS AND SCROLL SAWS The band saw's blade is a big metal continuous loop, or band, with saw teeth on one edge. When the power is on, the band travels around two or three wheels inside the band saw, with a small part of the blade exposed. The saw teeth face the woodworker, and the woodworker keeps the wood's face flat on the table as he or she pushes it slowly through the blade. A scroll saw

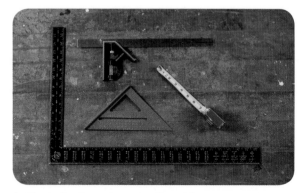

▲ Clockwise from the top: adjustable square, tape measure, framing square, and, in the center, speed square.

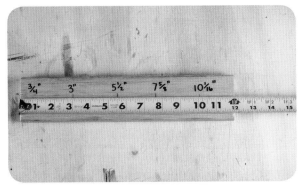

▲ The lines on a tape measure indicate the distance from the end of the tape measure, and in this case, the left end of this board. To measure from the end of a board, hook the metal end of the tape measure over the board's end. The longest lines on a tape measure indicate whole numbers; the number nearest these longest lines is the distance, in inches, from the end. The second-longest lines, the half-inch marks, are halfway between the whole number marks (the 5½-inch mark is shown). After that come the quarter-inch marks (there are four quarters in an inch: count from the left to see how many quarters your measurement is; the ¾-inch mark is shown). The next lines are eighths (the 7⅝-inch mark is shown). On this ruler, the smallest lines are sixteenths (the 10¹/₁₆-inches mark is shown).

is similar to a band saw, but its blade operates with an up-and-down motion. See page 29 for more information.

CIRCULAR SAW Like a miter saw, a circular saw has a round blade, but a circular saw is handheld, and the wood you're working with is clamped to the edge of the work surface while you move the circular saw along the wood to cut it. Although a circular saw can be used to cut wood to length in a setting where using a miter saw is not possible, it is more difficult to make an accurate cut with a portable power tool than with a stationary machine. The circular saw is not used frequently in this book. See page 31 for more information.

COPING SAW A coping saw is the manual version of a band saw, but it's more versatile because it can cut any angle (this will come in handy when fitting the arms on the International Orange chair). Use a coping saw to cut

▲ Two band saw blades, each with a different width. Both blades can cut curves, but the narrower blade can cut smaller curves. The wider blade has less of a tendency to break and handles straighter lines better.

▲ Band saws and scroll saws cut wood much like a sewing machine sews fabric: the wood is pushed through by the woodworker's hands while the blade stays at a single point.

curves or unusual shapes. See page 29 for more information.

JIGSAW The handheld power version of a band saw, a jigsaw can be used to cut curved lines, or, using a jig as a guide, straight lines. It is less accurate than a band saw, but can be used when a project cannot be maneuvered into a band saw. See page 30 for more information.

MITER SAW A stationery machine that's connected to a power source, a miter saw (sometimes spelled *mitre saw*) may also be referred to as chop saw. The miter saw that I used for the projects in this book is a compound miter saw, which means that in addition to being able to rotate the blade to cut 45-degree angles, called miters, the blade can also be angled to cut bevels—a slope from the top to the back face of the board. My miter saw has a 10-inch blade, which means nominally 1 × 8 and wider boards need to be cut in two steps. A sliding compound miter saw, while generally more expensive than a compound miter saw, has the capacity to cut wide pieces of wood with a single cut.

You'll use a miter saw for every project in this book, and most of the cuts you'll make will be 90 degrees, but the saw can also be adjusted to angle either the face or the edge of the board. You'll learn about making angled cuts in the projects that require them. See page 27 for more information.

Drilling Tools

DRILL/DRIVER A cordless drill/driver is a power tool that you hold in your hand. Drill/drivers accomplish two tasks with one tool: they drill holes and they drive in screws. A

Miter Box

The miter saw's cousin, the miter box, is a guide for those patient woodworkers who choose to use a hand saw. The piece of wood to be cut is placed and clamped inside the box, which is stationary, and the saw is moved through two slots in the box's walls to ensure the correct angle. Miter boxes have slots for 90-degree and 45-degree angle cuts; some have additional angles. Woodworkers who prefer using hand tools rather than power tools would use a miter box to make angled cuts. If you are a very patient person who dislikes the noise of the miter saw, give it a try.

handheld drill/driver can drill holes with any bit as long as the bit fits in the drill/driver's chuck (the device that holds it in place), but you don't have as much control, especially when using larger drill bits. Use a drill/driver for predrilling holes for screws, or when the project is too big to be held or clamped on the table of the drill press. See page 39 for more information.

DRILL PRESS A stationary machine that stands on the floor or on a work surface, a drill press drills holes that are identical every time, so you don't have to worry about the bit wobbling around. Use a drill press to drill holes for dowels, as in the bistro table project; to use a hole saw, as in the plant shelf project; or for any hole that needs to be precise. For most of the projects in this book, you won't need to use a drill press, but if you plan on continuing woodworking, I recommend buying one. See page 33 for more information.

Other Indispensable Tools

CLAMPS Clamps are used to hold two pieces of wood together, or to secure a piece of wood or an assembly to the work surface. They can also be used to provide a stationary stop to push against while you're screwing pieces together. I recommend having several on hand for projects.

DOWELS Small poles made of wood, dowels are useful as a spacing guide. A dowel with a ¾-inch diameter will fit snugly in a hole drilled by a ¾-inch drill bit.

HAMMER Hammers are used to drive in nails.

JIG Any tool you make as a template, guide, or location marker is called a jig.

MALLET A large wooden hammer with a rubber head, mallets are usually used to hammer on wood because they're softer and won't dent the wood. Don't use a mallet for driving in nails, because it will end up dented.

PENCILS Marking measurements on boards is necessary: you'll need to mark the locations of holes, the edges of cuts, and the location of boards being screwed in to. The type of pencil you use to mark your boards is a matter of personal preference. Many woodworkers prefer carpenter's pencils, which have flat sides and won't roll off a work surface. The flat lead can be sharpened to a very fine edge, to precisely mark a line, and the wide, flat surface of the lead can be used to write lightly enough so that the lead doesn't make a groove on the board. Most carpenter's pencils will not fit into a conventional pencil sharpener, so they must be sharpened by hand with a knife; you can also lay a piece of sandpaper on the work surface and use it to sharpen your pencil as long as you don't mind getting a little graphite smudge on the next board.

Generally, I make marks on wood lightly with a mechanical pencil. Although it isn't as traditional, elegant, or precise, it's faster. I find that taking time away from building to hand-sharpen a pencil takes me out of the flow of woodworking.

PUSH STICK If you need to control the part of the wood that's close to the blade, use a piece of scrap wood called a push stick to keep your hands away from the blade. Push

▲ A push stick (right) is an indispensable safety tool, and it's a tool that you can make yourself. Use them to push the wood through the blade to avoid putting your hand near the blade.

sticks come in all shapes and sizes, but yours doesn't have to be fancy—you only need a piece of scrap wood with a notch cut out of one corner.

SANDERS Handheld power sanders include palm sanders and random orbital sanders. They're portable and used to shape and smooth edges and surfaces. See page 37 for more information.

SANDPAPER Sandpaper comes in many grits; for outdoor furniture, you'll need 60-grit, 80-grit, and 100- or even 120-grit sandpaper to make your boards' faces soft (for outdoor furniture, I usually end with 80- or 100-grit sandpaper for bench surfaces and armrests). Sandpaper comes in 9 × 11-inch sheets, which you can fold or tear into quarter sizes.

With any outdoor project, start with a low-grit sandpaper and end with a high-grit sandpaper. Low numbers are grittier and remove more wood, but they leave marks. You can erase the marks with a higher-grit sandpaper. Start with 60-grit for leveling joints and taking away deep scratches. If the joints look great and there aren't any significant scratches, start with 80-grit sandpaper to round the edges and make the plugs level (feel the joints and plugs with your eyes closed; if you can't tell where they are with your fingers, then you're finished sanding them flush). Go over everything you've done with each higher grit of sandpaper until you are satisfied with the smoothness of your project.

Don't waste your time by wearing out a piece of sandpaper within an inch of its life. Replace sandpaper as soon as it starts to feel dull compared with a fresh sheet of the same grit. See page 36 for more information.

Staying Organized

I use a permanent marker and green masking tape to make labels to indicate the name of each board, such as backrest, armrest, or leg, and so on, for projects that are constructed from many pieces. The bold writing is easy to read when I'm trying to locate a wayward piece of wood, the marker doesn't dent the wood, and the ink won't smudge off the tape onto the board.

When I'm finished working on a large project for the day, I often tape similar pieces together for storage. The next time I come into the shop, I'll have neat piles of wood that are already sorted and I'll never lose a board.

Build Your Skills

The best way to learn how to use tools and machines, particularly ones that can be dangerous, is to learn directly from another person. She or he can recognize if you are doing something incorrectly and correct your movement. If you have never used one of these tools or machines, I urge you to seek guidance from an experienced woodworker the first few times you use it.

You do not need to own all of these tools and machines. For every project, you will need a miter saw and a drill/driver. Read each list of tools and materials completely before starting to build to see what you'll need. There are many ways to perform the same operation. Generally, stationary machines make more accurate cuts, while handheld portable power tools can perform operations on wood pieces or assemblies that may not fit into, or would be awkward to bring to, a stationary machine. In a pinch, most of these tools can be replaced, with varying degrees of accuracy, by hand tools.

Here, you will find only the most basic instructions for woodworking machine and tool operation. Each machine manufacturer and model operates slightly differently—as you become more comfortable with your own machine, you'll learn everything it can do.

Safety First: General rules for safety in the workshop

Before undertaking any woodworking project, review the important safety guidelines below. There are many versions of eye, ear, and lung protection for different applications. Make sure you're using protection products made specifically for woodworking.

BE ALERT Each time you are about to enter your workspace, ask yourself whether you are in a proper mental state for woodworking. Alert, unhurried, calm woodworkers turn out better projects with no injuries. You will have a natural, healthy fear of moving machinery. Listen calmly to this fear: learn how the machine moves, work slowly, and never get close to the blade. You are in control of the machine.

KEEP YOUR WORKSPACE CLEAN AND SAFE Sawdust, off-cuts of wood, and shavings accumulate quickly and can become a fire hazard as well as a slipping hazard, so sweep your workspace regularly. Arrange extension cords in such a way that they will not be tripped over. Have enough work surface available for the project materials, tools, machines, and instructions.

ANTICIPATE PROBLEMS If the piece of wood you are cutting goes flying, which way will it fly? If the wood slips forward into the blade, will your hand slip into the blade as well? Will any part of your clothing get caught in moving machinery?

KEEP YOUR EYES ON YOUR WORK AT ALL TIMES If something else catches your attention, turn the power off and then look away from your work.

KNOW WHEN TO TURN OFF THE MACHINE Before you reach anywhere near a moving blade to remove cut pieces, turn the machine off and wait for the blade to stop moving. When you're making an adjustment that requires your hands to be on or near the blade, unplug the power cord.

PROTECT YOUR EYES Every time you make a cut or perform any operation that could cause a piece of wood to fly off, wear safety glasses. Regular prescription glasses will not protect your eyes. If you wear prescription glasses, wear safety glasses that fit over them. (The safety glasses pictured fit over my glasses.)

PROTECT YOUR EARS Usually, if a woodworking machine or tool needs to be plugged in during use, it is loud enough to warrant using ear protection. Earmuffs, like the ones shown, are my hearing protection of choice because they're big, bright, and therefore difficult to lose. Disposable foam earplugs are another option; squeeze them before placing in your ears—they will expand to fit. It takes a few tries to get used to them. There are also gel plugs that come on a band you wear around the back of your head (or around your neck when not in use), which are much less bulky than muff-style hearing protection, and last longer than disposable foam plugs (although you will need to buy replacement gel plugs).

PROTECT YOUR LUNGS Sawing and sanding wood produces a lot of dust. Wear a dust mask whenever you're making dust.

DON'T WEAR ANYTHING THAT DANGLES Long hair, earrings, hoodie pull cords, and floppy long sleeves are all hell-bent on getting themselves violently caught in running machines. Dash their dreams of dragging you into grisly injury by removing, tying, or tucking them away.

PROTECT YOUR FEET Do not wear sandals, heels, or open-toed shoes in your workspace. Imagine dropping a large piece of wood on a toe. If your reaction might be some unprintable word followed by a trip to the hospital, change into boots with hard tops. Make sure any shoes you wear into the workshop have solid soles that can stomp, carefree, over upturned screws and splinters lurking on your wood shop floor.

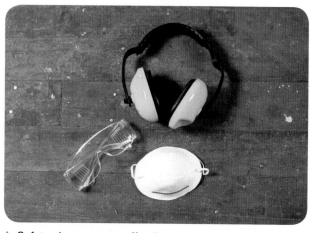

▲ Safety glasses, ear muffs, disposable dust mask.

How to Use a Miter Saw

▲ A miter saw with the blade raised. When it's not being used, the miter saw's blade mechanism can be locked down into its table.

▲ To unlock the blade mechanism, hold the handle on the top of the saw with your left hand and pull the pin on the back of the saw with your right hand. The blade mechanism will lift into place.

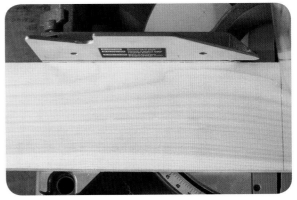

▲ Place the wood flat on the miter saw's table, and flat against the miter saw's fence (the vertical piece on the far side of the table).

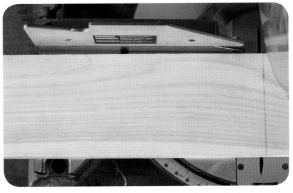

▲ This piece of wood is not flat against the miter saw's fence.

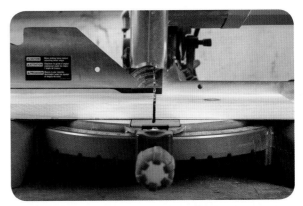

▲ When the wood is cut, it cuts away the thickness of the blade, called a kerf. Therefore, mark boards to be cut one at a time; otherwise, the boards will be too short.

▲ With the power off, slide the board under the blade so that the penciled line is directly under the blade. Know which side of the board you are going to keep, and slide the board toward the "keep" side until the very edge of the blade's teeth are touching the line.

▼ With the power still off, bring the blade mechanism down so it is touching the wood. Look closely at the blade to make sure the teeth are just touching the outside of the line.

▲ Hold the wood firmly in place with your left hand. (The board can also be clamped in place: if you're using a clamp to hold the wood, place your left hand on the wood or on the work surface in front of the saw so it has somewhere to be while your brain is focused on cutting the wood.) The central part of the miter saw's table is a semicircle: your hand should always be outside of the semicircle when the blade is moving. Stand a little to the left of center—if a piece of wood flies off, it will be on the right side, where you are not holding the wood. Turn the power on; usually there are two switches on the handle of the blade mechanism, operated by your thumb and forefinger, that have to be engaged.

▲ Slowly lower the blade mechanism down through the wood until it can't go any farther. Then let the blade mechanism lift itself up and let go of the power switches. After the blade completely stops turning, you may move your hands off the saw and reach for your wood.

How to Use a Band Saw

To cut a curve using a band saw, first draw the curve on the wood. Using the knob on the right side of the machine, adjust the height of the blade guard so it is just over the height of the wood, but far up enough for you to see where the blade enters the wood.

▲ Align the penciled line with the band saw's blade.

▼ Hold the wood with both hands, keeping your fingers away from the blade. Be sure the wood's face is flat on the table. Slowly push the wood through, turning the wood as needed to keep the cut on the curve.

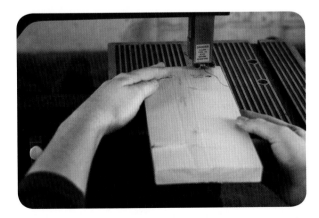

Using a Band Saw: Go Slowly

In the projects in this book, most of what you'll be cutting using a band saw won't have tight curves. Even so, it pays to go slowly—cutting too-tight curves, especially when moving fast, results either in the blade breaking or falling off its wheels. Either way, you'll hear a pop and the machine will stop cutting. If this happens, turn off the machine and wait for the sound of the moving wheels to stop before you open the covers. Everybody breaks band saw blades; keep a few extras on hand to replace the broken ones.

How to Use a Coping Saw

A coping saw's teeth are angled and will do almost all the cutting on the pull stroke. The wood will cut more slowly than you expect. Adopt a patient, Zen-like attitude when you're working with a coping saw, because the quality of your cut will depend on it. If you rush through the cut, it will turn out ragged or slanted. Make a few practice cuts on a piece of scrap wood to see what cutting curves by hand feels like and to see if your cuts are angled.

▲ Clamp the wood to the workbench so that the end of the wood with the line you'll be cutting extends off the workbench. If you want the cut to be 90 degrees from the face, be sure to hold the blade perfectly vertical, not tilted. (If cutting a vertical line is easier for you, the wood can also be clamped in a vise.)

▲ Here's an example of two curves, one cut by hand with a coping saw (left) and the other cut with a band saw (right). The cut made with the coping saw is slightly angled, because I didn't realize I wasn't holding the blade straight up and down. In a situation like this, use sandpaper to make the angled cut identical to the good cut.

How to Use a Jigsaw

▲ To cut a straight line, clamp a jig board (a straight piece of wood that you can use as a guide) on top of the board you are cutting. The line you are cutting should be positioned off the edge of the work surface, not on the work surface, and the edge of the jig board should be positioned so that it is the same distance from the line you're cutting as the distance from the blade to the edge of the jigsaw's base plate.

▼ Keep the edge of the jigsaw's base plate next to the edge of the jig board as you move the saw along the wood.

How to Use a Circular Saw

▲ To cut a long, straight line along the length of a board, clamp a straight piece of scrap wood at least as long as your cut to the face of the board and to the work surface. The distance from the edge of the scrap board to the line you're cutting should be the same as the distance from the edge of the saw's blade to the outer edge of the base plate.

This jig can be clamped to the work surface in a spot that is a certain distance from the miter saw's blade. This is called setting a stop. You can place one board after another against the stop and cut boards that are always the exact same length, saving yourself from having to measure every piece first. With a stop, you only have to measure the first board, position the stop, and then cut the boards. Make sure the miter saw's feet are also clamped or bolted to the work surface so the miter saw doesn't vibrate around, making your multiple cuts different lengths.

How to Make a Jig

▲ I made this small L-shaped jig to use with my miter saw. The height from the work surface to my miter saw's table is the same as the width of a 1 × 4, so I screwed two 1 × 4 pieces together, edge to face.

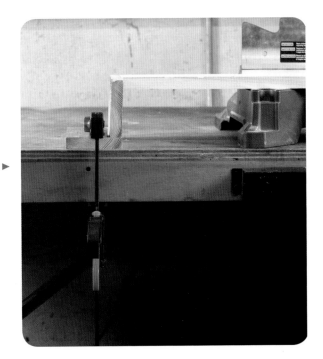

▶

▲ If I have a long board that needs to be held up so it doesn't flop down after it's cut, I can place the wider part of the jig on the work surface and lay the board on top of it.

How to Use a Clamp

Any time you use a handheld tool, the board will need to be kept stationary. Clamp the board securely to the work surface or clamp the board to the piece of furniture you are attaching it to. You can also tighten a clamp to the work surface at one end of a board (don't clamp the board itself) to have something to push against when screwing two boards together—this is called setting a cleat.

There are many types of clamps, and it's helpful to have more clamps than you think you'll need. For the projects in this book, you'll need at least four or five. I mostly used one-handed bar clamps.

▲ One-handed bar clamps have a release mechanism that can be pushed to slide the lower jaw up and down the bar.

▲ When the jaw is in place, squeeze the trigger a few times until the clamp is firmly holding the wood pieces. When you're finished using the clamp, press the release mechanism again and the clamp will loosen.

Chuck

A chuck (noun) is the device on a drill press or drill/driver that holds the drill bit in place. To "chuck" (verb) means to "tighten the chuck around the drill bit."

How to Use a Drill Press

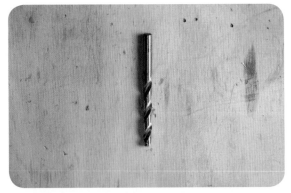

▲ Drill bits come in a range of sizes. The smooth part of the drill bit is called the shank, and the part with the twists is called the body. The diameter of the drill bit is its size.

▲ Insert the chuck key into one of the holes in the side of the chuck until the gears are engaged, and use it to further tighten the chuck around the drill bit.

▲ Drill bits are held in place by the chuck. To install the drill bit, rotate the chuck until the jaws open wide enough to snugly fit the bit. Place the bit, pointy end down, in the chuck, and tighten the chuck with your hand.

▲ The drill bit's smooth part, the shank, should be inside the chuck, and the body, the part with the twists, should be exposed.

▲ Hold one of the handles on the feed lever to move the drill bit up and down.

▲ To move the table up and down, loosen the release lock on the left side of the drill press.

▽ Next, turn the crank, if there is one, on the right side clockwise to move the table up and counterclockwise to move it down.

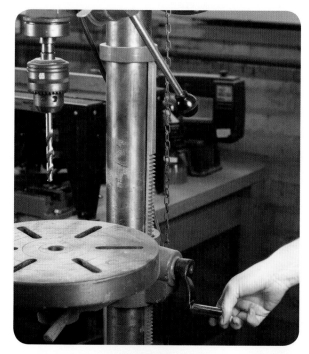

Holding the bit all the way down, position the table. If you are drilling a hole that goes all the way through the wood, called a through-hole, the drill bit should end below the surface of the table. If you've placed a sacrificial board underneath the board you are drilling (which is a good idea, because it prevents tear-out, or ragged edges, where the drill bit exits the hole), and you're drilling a through-hole, the drill bit will enter the sacrificial board. ▶

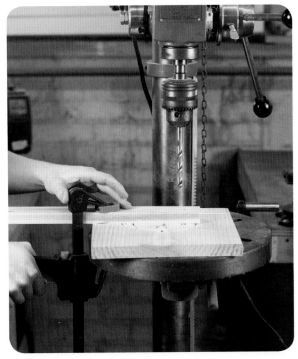

▲ With the drill press off, position the wood flat on the sacrificial board under the drill bit. Move the drill bit down toward the face of the wood and move the wood until its mark is centered beneath the point of the drill bit. The wood is now in place to be drilled: you may clamp it to the sacrificial board and the table of the drill press, or simply hold it in place with your hand at least 2 inches away from the path of the drill bit.

▲ When the wood is in place and the drill bit is in the up position, turn on the power. Slowly move the feed lever all the way down into the wood until you feel it stop moving, and lift it up all the way. Then turn the power off.

▲ A hole drilled using a drill press.

How to Use a Sanding Block

Well-done sanding can hide misaligned joints, make a piece look more professional, and even make a project last longer.

◀ Sanding surfaces, corners, and edges by hand is easier with a sanding block. Fold or tear 9 × 11-inch sheets of sandpaper into quarters and wrap them around the sanding block. Be sure to wear a mask when you're sanding to avoid inhaling dust.

◀ To create a chamfer, or angled edge, keep your hand at a 45-degree angle from the wood's surfaces.

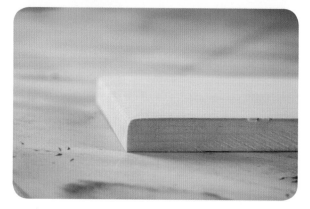

◀ To create a roundover, or rounded edge, rotate your hand when you're sanding a corner.

How to Use a Palm Sander

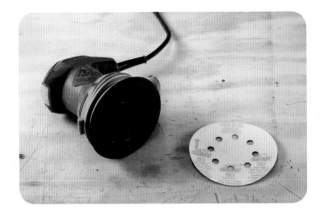

▲ Palm sanders are fantastic time-savers. This is a random orbit palm sander. Attach specially made discs of sandpaper to its flat circular surface and replace them as necessary. Palm sanders also come with square bottoms—using the levers on either side of the sander, attach a quarter of a sheet of 9 × 11-inch sandpaper to its surface.

Sanding produces a lot of dust. Wear a dust mask, and use the small dust-collection bag that comes with the sander, or better yet, attach the sander to a vacuum hose.

▲ Many random orbit sanders use sandpaper with hook-and-loop backing: just stick it on, aligning the dust-collector holes, and rip it off like Velcro to replace.

The method I use for attaching boards together involves counterboring holes for the screws and inserting a wood plug that sits flush with the face of the board to cover the hole and protect the screw.

This technique may be different from other methods you've seen. At first glance, it may seem like a lot of steps, but by marking and predrilling pilot holes for the screws, you'll avoid having screws sticking out of or splitting the wood. When the project is assembled, you'll fill the counterbored holes with plugs and sand them so that they are flush with the wood. This gives the piece an elegant, finished look and protects the screw.

Almost all the structural screws used in this book are no. 8 deck screws (the 8 is a gauge number that refers to the diameter of the screw). In general, for nominally 1-inch-thick (actually ¾-inch-thick) wood, use 1¼-inch-long screws when you're attaching two pieces of flat stacked wood, and use 1⅝-inch-long screws when attaching two boards at a 90-degree angle. Buy one small box of each screw size and replenish as necessary. For more information on buying screws, see page 19.

Measuring and Marking Locations for Screw Holes

For the projects in this book, when two boards need to be joined together, I use a simple method of tracing the end of one ¾-inch-thick (nominally 1 inch thick) board onto the end of the board it's being joined with to mark a rectangular area where the holes should go. Typically, two screws are used for every board that is attached to the end of another board. The positions of the screw holes should bisect the rectangle lengthwise and be equidistant from the both ends of the rectangle. The locations of the screws are usually clearly visible in the photos, providing you with additional guidance.

If you want to double-check the position of the screw holes, measure from two sides of the rectangle; for example, once from the edge of the board and once from the end. Draw a line from each side; where the lines cross is the point where the screw hole should be predrilled.

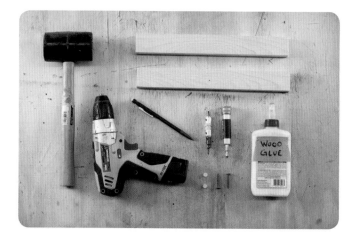

▲ From left: rubber mallet, drill/driver, mechanical pencil, wood, countersink bit, quick-flip drive, wood plugs, #8 deck screws, wood glue.

Making Perfect Seams

The trick to getting tight joints (in this case, a perfect seam) is to feel the edges of both pieces of wood with the fingers of your non-dominant hand as you are driving the screw with your dominant hand. Drive the screw until the two pieces of wood appear to be sucked into each other. A perfect seam cannot be felt with your fingertips when your eyes are closed—it will be indiscernable. Slightly misaligned but tight seams can be sanded to perfection.

Making Plugs

To make plugs, slice pieces about ⅛ inch long from a dowel with a ⁵⁄₁₆-inch diameter using a band saw. Use a push stick to hold the end of the dowel that's closest to the blade. You can also make plugs using use a plug cutter attachment for a drill press on a ⅛-inch-thick craft board.

Countersink Bits

A countersink bit has two ends: one for predrilling the counterbored hole, and one for driving the screw. Either end can be removed for replacing or, in the case of the ¹¹⁄₆₄-inch drill bit, adjusting the depth of the screw hole, using the tiny hex screwdriver at the end of the quick-flip drive.

How to Counterbore and Plug Holes

▲ A quick-flip drive holds the countersink bit. This one has a brass ring that can be popped away from you to insert and remove the countersink bit, or popped toward you to lock the bit in place. Hold the quick-flip drive in your left (or non-dominant) hand and the countersink bit in your right hand. With your left thumb and forefinger, push the brass ring away from you until you feel it click into the outer position. The outer part will easily come out of the shank. There are two ends to this outer part: the drilling end, with the ¹¹⁄₆₄-inch drill bit, and the driving end, with the Phillips or square bit.

▲ Insert the countersink bit, with the ¹¹⁄₆₄-inch drill bit facing outward, into the shank of the quick-flip drive. You may need to turn it a little so the hex in the center of the countersink bit engages. Pull the brass ring toward you to lock the bit in place.

▲ Turn the chuck in the drill/driver so that it opens enough for the quick-flip drive to fit into.

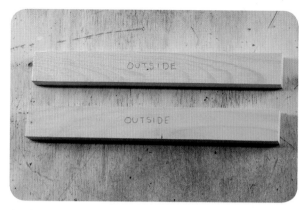

▲ I've written "outside" on one face of both pieces of wood and "inside" on the other side of both pieces of wood. We'll screw the end of one of the board's faces to the end of the other board.

▲ Insert the quick-flip drive and tighten the chuck. Press the forward-facing arrow button, which is usually on the side of the drill/driver. This makes the drill turn forward when you press the trigger. When you need to reverse a screw, you can change the direction to reverse on the other side of the drill.

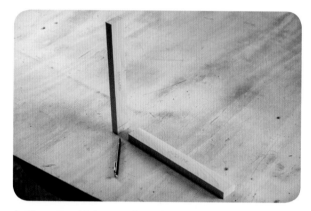

▲ Trace the thickness of one board onto the other board's outside face. You'll have a line that's ¾ inch from the end. Make two dots, midway between the penciled line and the end of the board and equidistant from the edges of the board. The dots mark the spots where you will predrill the counter-bored holes, or make pilot holes. You'll generally want to use at least two screws, even on a narrow board, because they will keep the joint from rotating.

▲ To predrill the counterbored holes, place the end of the drill bit on one of the dots, making sure you are holding the drill/driver straight, or at a 90-degree angle from the board. Hold the board with your other hand or clamp it to the work surface. Pull the trigger on the drill/driver and push firmly until the drill bit has disappeared into the board, until the drill bit reaches a point just a little above the triangular tip. With the trigger still depressed, pull the drill straight out. (If the drill rocks too much, it could break off the bit inside the wood.)

Sacrificial Boards

If you don't want to drill into the work surface, place a scrap board, commonly called a sacrificial board, underneath the board you are drilling. The drill bit will drill into the sacrificial board instead of the work surface.

▲ You'll be left with a small hole all the way through the wood with a larger hole on the surface. This is a counterbored hole. Drill the other hole in the same way. You'll have two counterbored holes.

▲ Attach a clamp to the work surface so you'll have a surface to push against when screwing. Place the two boards on the work surface, with the outside where the screws will go close to the edge. Be sure both outside faces are on the outside. I laid the face of one board and the end of the other board on the work surface, but if it is more comfortable for you, you can also place both boards on their edges.

▲ Flip the quick-flip drive so the drive end is out. Push the brass piece away from you until it clicks.

▲ Pull the drill bit out and flip it around.

◀ Insert it back into the quick-flip drive and pull the brass piece toward you until it clicks.

Troubleshooting Joints

If the joint is loose, meaning the two boards are not sucked up tightly to one another, you may need to apply more force when driving the screws. If the joint is not at a 90-degree angle, reverse out the screws using the reverse button on the drill/driver, hold the boards together firmly, put the drill/driver back in forward, and screw the boards together again. If the boards are still not at 90 degrees, reverse the screw out, predrill another counterbored hole next to the bad one, and put a screw in the new hole. When it's time to plug the holes, plug all of them and the bad hole without a screw will be unnoticeable.

▲ Use the fingers of your non-dominant hand to hold the corners of both boards in alignment. With the drill/driver still in forward, drive the screws into place.

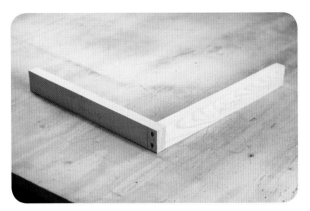

▲ The heads of the screws should be below the surface of the board and the two boards should be firmly attached.

Stripped Screws

Is a screw not moving, or moving slower than the turning drill/driver? Does it sound like a helicopter? Are tiny shards of metal appearing on the head of the screw? If any of these things are happening, the screw is being stripped. Before damaging the screw to the point where it gets stuck halfway in the wood, reverse it out, throw it away, and try again with a new screw, pushing harder this time.

Repairing Cracks

If the wood cracks when a screw is being driven into it, leave the screw in place, use a piece of paper to dab some glue in the crack, and use a clamp to close the crack. If the screw is in deep enough to do so, it may help to reverse the screw out about a half turn until the wood comes back together.

▲ When the project is finished and you're sure you don't want to make any changes, put a small drop of glue in each screw hole and insert the plugs.

▲ Gently pound the plugs into the holes with a mallet. Sand the plugs until they're flush with the surface of the wood.

▲ Close-up of a plug, as it appears
on the flower box project.

Finishing Touches: Staining and Painting

There are many options for finishing and painting outdoor projects. As long as the paint or stain is labeled as being suitable for exteriors, you're all set. I prefer water-based products because they're not a fire, health, or environmental hazard. Many people prefer oil-based paints and stains because they have a richer, deeper look. As long as you use them safely, either is fine. Follow the cleanup instructions on the containers.

SPRAY PAINT AND SPRAY FINISH Wear gloves. Shake the can well. Start and finish your spray off the edge of the wood. Imagine the cone of the spray coming out of the nozzle in thirds: the center of the circle is one third, and the "overspray" is the outer two thirds. Spray paint or finish onto wood in rows, starting with only one third of overspray on the outermost edge of the wood. Start the next row with the center of the circle on the first line of overspray, and start the third row with the center of the circle on the previous overspray. Repeat rows all over the outside surface, then spray the inside surfaces.

OIL- OR WATER-BASED STAIN Wear gloves. Because it enhances rather than hides the grain, nuances, and mistakes in your project, stain is the least forgiving way to complete a project and, many would argue, the most beautiful. Fill any gaps, holes, or gouges with wood filler that matches the color of the wood and, when dry, sand the filler until it's flush with the surface. Every part of your project should be sanded with the same grit, starting with low-grit sandpaper and working your way up to finer grits, such as 100 or 120. After sanding, apply pre-stain wood conditioner and let it dry. Stain can be applied with a brush and wiped off with a rag, or simply applied with a rag. Clear polyurethane also looks fantastic, either over a stain or on its own.

OIL- OR WATER-BASED PAINT Wear gloves for oil-based paint. Brush paint on the project, always keeping a wet edge, that is, never letting the edge of the paint dry, creating a seam before you brush on more. Use a broad brush for wide faces and a narrower brush for hard-to-reach places.

CLEANUP Oil-based paints and stains need to be cleaned from paintbrushes with solvents. The manufacturer's directions will generally call for using mineral spirits, paint thinner, turpentine, or acetone. These solvents cannot be washed down the drain, so keep a waste container available. The waste can be disposed of at a hazardous-materials collection facility, or left to separate so the clear liquid on top can be skimmed off and sealed in a glass jar to be used again. The remaining sludge can be dried out with sawdust or kitty litter and thrown away. Rags soaked with oil products or cleaning solvents should never be crumpled up or stacked—immerse them in a sealed container of water before disposing of them so they don't combust.

Part Two

PROJECTS

▲ This is a classic Shaker pegboard. Shaker pegboards can be built with or without shelves, with any number or kind of pegs. The black pieces were painted before assembly.

Shaker Pegboard Shelf

20 in. wide × 10¾ in. high × 5½ in. deep

According to Shaker philosophy, the simpler and more efficient a design is, the closer it is to heaven. The Shaker pegboard shelf is an icon of Shaker design. I can't think of anything more heavenly than an uncluttered indoor workspace, but a pegboard is also excellent for an outdoor space—it's the perfect place to hang gardening gloves, rest tools, or dry herbs.

A Shaker pegboard is a terrific first project—you'll use the basic operations needed in almost every project in this book: measuring, cutting, drilling, screwing, and sanding.

Pegboards can be designed with or without shelves and in any shape, size, or proportion. You can make a board with a single peg, or make a long peg rail with multiple pegs for lining a wall, fence, or shed. Pegs can be purchased at craft shops and hardware stores. Most Shaker pegs are made of birch; they are stronger than pine and more suitable for holding heavy items. If you like, use any kind of hook, knob, or cut-out shape instead of traditional pegs. Instead of making the shelf top rectangular, make any shape you please. Making pegboards is a fantastic use of your scrap wood and your imagination.

MATERIALS

One 1 in. × 3 in. × 4 ft. board

One 1 in. × 6 in. × 4 ft. board

Paint (optional)

Three Shaker pegs with a ½-in. diameter base

Eight 1⅝-in. no. 8 deck screws

Weatherproof wood glue

Plugs

TOOLS

Miter saw

Adjustable square

Band saw, jigsaw, or coping saw

Clamps

Tape measure

Drill press

Drill/driver

Quick-flip drive with a #8 ¹¹⁄₆₄-in. countersink bit

½-in.-diameter drill bit

Rubber mallet

Sander and sandpaper

1 Using a miter saw, cut all three pieces to length and sand.

Using the miter saw, cut the 1 × 3 board to 14 in. long; this piece is the pegboard. One 1 × 6 board should be cut into two pieces: one 20 in. long, for the shelf; and one 10 in. long, for the side supports. Sand all the pieces except for the ends of the 10-in. side support and the 14-in. pegboard piece—they will be screwed to other pieces.`

2 Paint selected pieces. (Optional)

If you are planning on sanding or painting the surface of the pegboard a different color from the pegs, do it now. If you wait until later, the inside corners will be more difficult to sand or paint. I chose to spray paint the shelf and the pegboard and leave the side supports and pegs unpainted.

3 Mark and cut the side supports.

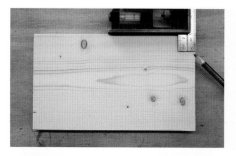

Set an adjustable square at 1 in. Measure in from both edges on opposite corners, and mark each end. Draw an S-curve from one mark to the other. It doesn't have to be perfectly symmetrical—you'll have a chance to finesse the shape later.

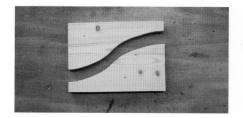

Using a band saw, jigsaw, or coping saw, cut along the line.

Place the smaller piece on top of the larger piece and trace the curve of the smaller piece onto the larger piece.

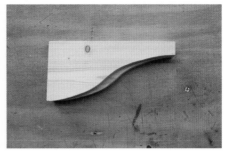

Using a band saw, jigsaw, or coping saw, cut along the line you traced onto the larger piece, making it the same size as the smaller piece.

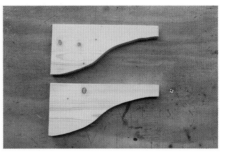

Use a clamp or a vise to secure both pieces together tightly between two sacrificial boards and sand them. Sanding them together will ensure that the curves are symmetrical. When both parts are sanded, unclamp them and lightly sand the corners.

4 Mark and drill the holes for the pegs.

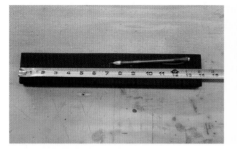

Using a tape measure, find the center of the length of the 14-in. pegboard and mark it. To be sure you've marked the exact center, measure from the other end as well.

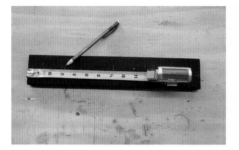

Mark 3 in. in from one end and 3 in. in from the other end.

Find the center of the width of the board and set the adjustable square at this distance.

Use the edge of the adjustable square to mark cross-lines on all three marks.

Chuck a ½-in. drill bit in a drill press or handheld drill/driver. Set the depth stop so the drill bit stops just before hitting the table, so it will go almost all the way through the wood, but not completely through. This leaves enough room for the peg to go in all the way and for any excess glue to pool at the bottom of the hole once you've pounded the peg in.

Drill holes at each of the three marks you've made.

Pound the pegs into the holes and predrill holes for attaching the pegboard to a wall.

Place a drop of glue into each hole and use a mallet to pound a peg into each hole. The pegs should go in the holes all the way up to their shoulders.

Predrill the holes needed to attach the pegboard to a wall. The adjustable square should still be set to half the width of the board; mark that distance at both ends of the pegboard, and cross the marks by the distance from the side. Using the quick-flip drive set to the $^{11}/_{64}$-in. drill bit end, predrill these two holes, but only up to the depth of the first cone on the drive, so when screws are inserted, they will sit flush with the surface of the board. (Place a sacrificial board under the pegboard, as seen in this photo, if you want to avoid drilling into the work surface.)

Mark and attach the side supports. 6

Arrange the pegboard on the work surface with all its pieces configured in a way that pleases you. The pegboard may be positioned close to the shelf or farther down.

Once you know where you want the pegboard positioned, trace one end of the pegboard onto one side support.

Then place the straight sides of both side supports next to each other on the work surface and continue the traced lines onto the other side support. It's important that the lines on the second side support be in the exact same place as on the first side support—a mirror image—so that the pegboard sits parallel to the shelf.

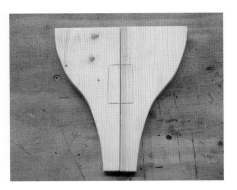

6 Mark and attach the side supports. (Continued)

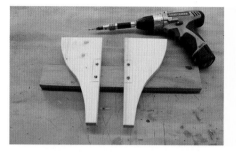

Mark two screw holes on each side support. Using the drill/driver with a ½-in. bit, predrill for four counterbored holes; that is, drill all the way up to the first cylinder on the quick-flip drive.

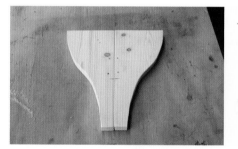

Turn both side supports over and mark a line below the lower hole where the bottom of the pegboard will abut the side supports. Use the bottom line on the inside face of the side support as a guide; it should essentially carry over to the outside face of the side support.

Place the pegboard on a corner of the work surface with one of the side supports abutting the work surface corner. Place a clamp at the other end of the pegboard (the one not abutting the work surface corner) so you'll have something to push against when you're driving in the screws.

Align the mark you've made on the inside face of the side support with the bottom of the pegboard. Using a drill/driver and 1⅝-in. screws, attach the first side support to the pegboard.

Turn the assembly around and position the other side support. Align the mark on the other side support with the bottom of the pegboard and screw the second side support into place.

Mark and attach the shelf.   7

Place the assembly on the work surface with the shelf on top. Use the adjustable square to center the shelf on the side supports by adjusting it slightly until both end measurements are the same.

7 **Mark and attach the shelf.** (Continued)

Trace the side supports onto the underside of the shelf.

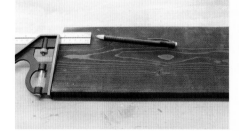

Mark for screw holes and predrill for counterbored holes.

Flip the shelf over and mark the same distance from the end of the shelf to the outside of the side supports so you can properly align the shelf.

Place the assembly on the corner of the work surface with a clamp at the end of one of the side supports. Align the shelf and screw it to one of the side supports. Move the assembly so the clamp can be at the end of the other side support and screw the shelf to the remaining side support.

Put a small drop of glue into each screw hole, insert a plug, and gently pound the plugs into the holes with a mallet. Sand the plugs so that they're flush with the surface of the wood. If you're using paint, touch up the paint.

▲ The trellis is mounted on a garden shed that's the same height. It's mounted to the shed's wall with 2-in. galvanized corner braces.

Trellis

41½ in. wide × 96 in. high × 1½ in. thick

One summer weekend, I went to the Connecticut shoreline to have a sunset picnic with friends. On our way, we walked past beach houses of all kinds; one of my favorites was a small, one-story 1940s cottage covered in hot pink roses. Lining the front of the house, supporting the roses, were sunburst-shaped trellises that looked like this one.

It took less than an hour and less than 10 dollars to build this trellis.

If the trellis is to be mounted to a fence or wall, mount it about 2 inches above the ground to prevent rot, and seal the ends with extra coats of paint. To give plants enough room to climb, attach the trellis 2 to 3 inches off a fence or wall using scrap wood or corner braces, or sturdily stake it in the ground so it's free-standing. Depending on the plant, you may want to use additional horizontal rails or eyehooks every 3 to 6 inches to provide an easy climb.

MATERIALS

Five 1 in. × 2 in. × 8 ft. boards

1½-in. no. 8 deck screws

Weatherproof wood glue

Plugs (optional; since this is a piece designed to be viewed from a distance and covered in leaves, the screw holes can be left unplugged)

Paint or stain (optional)

TOOLS

Miter saw

Tape measure

Speed square

Drill/driver

Quick-flip drive with a #8 $^{11}\!/_{64}$-in countersink bit

Rubber mallet (if you're using plugs)

1 Label and cut the five boards.

Using a pencil, label the end of each piece 1, 2, 3, 4, and 5. Using a miter saw, cut pieces 1 and 5 to 64 in. These pieces are two of the stiles of the trellis. Save the scrap. Cut pieces 2 and 4 to 80 in. These pieces are the other two stiles of the trellis. Save the scrap.

The four pieces of scrap wood, two at 32 in. and two at 16 in., are the horizontal pieces, or rails.

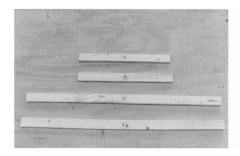

Use a tape measure to find and mark the center of each rail for predrilling one hole in each rail. Predrill one hole in each spot you marked.

2 Screw rails into stile number 3.

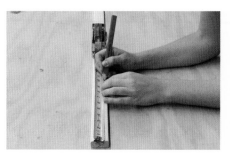

Using a tape measure, mark 10 in. up from the bottom of the longest piece, stile number 3.

Using a speed square to ensure a 90-degree angle, place one 16-in. rail with its lower edge on the line you have drawn. Using the drill/driver, screw the rail into place.

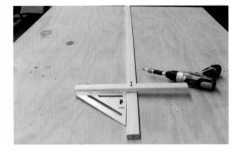

Mark 16 in. up from the top of the rail you just screwed in place. Screw the other 16-in. rail in place with its lower edge on the new line you've drawn, double-checking the 90-degree angle with the speed square.

Mark 16 in. up from the top of the second rail. Screw the 32-in. rail in place with its lower edge on the line you have drawn, double-checking the 90-degree angle with the speed square.

Mark 16 in. up from the top of the third rail and attach the remaining 32-in. rail, double-checking the 90-degree angle with the speed square.

3 Attach stiles 1 and 5.

On the work surface, arrange stiles 1 and 5 so their bottom ends touch the end of stile 3. The ends should intersect with the outer edges of the third rail from the bottom.

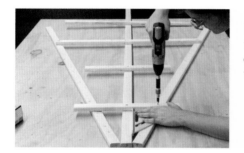

Place a speed square on the intersection of stile 3 and the lower rail to ensure the angle stays at 90 degrees when you attach the outer stile.

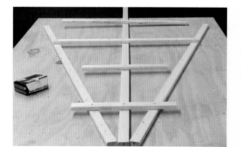

Predrill and attach all four intersections between stiles 1 and 3 and the rails with 1½-in. screws. The assembly should now look like this.

Slide stiles 2 and 4 under the rails all the way until their corners hit the other stiles. Position them halfway between the center stile 3 and the outer stiles.

Using a speed square from stile 3 to the unattached rails, predrill and screw all intersections that haven't yet been attached.

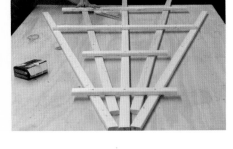

The finished assembly will have five vertical stiles and four horizontal rails.

5

If you're using plugs, put a small drop of glue into each screw hole, insert a plug, and gently pound the plugs into the holes with a mallet. Sand the plugs so that they're flush with the surface of the wood. Paint or stain.

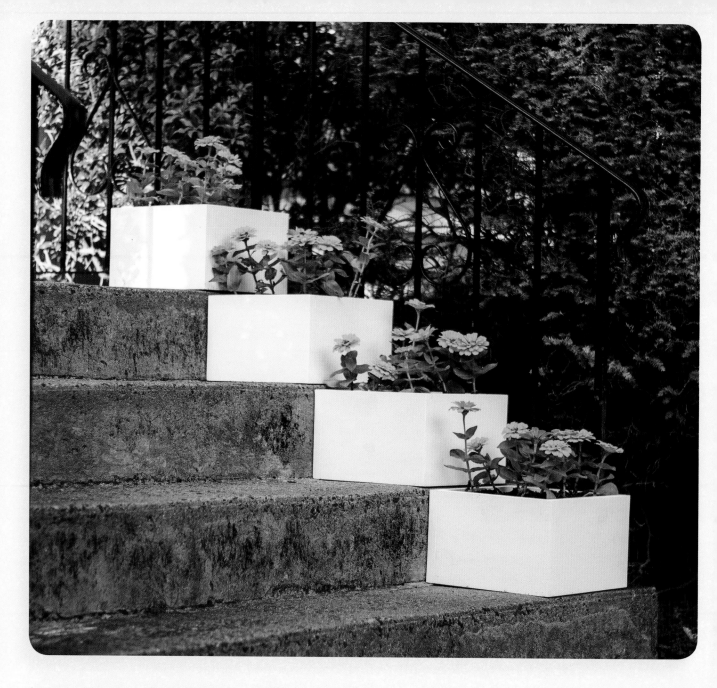

▲ A cascade of boxes echoes the shape of staircase.
Squares provide a simple geometric impact, and
well-sanded joints create a seamless effect.

Stair Box Planters

11½ in. wide × 11½ in. deep × 7¼ in. high

These sleek, simple boxes running down the side of a staircase echo the rise of the steps. They can be planted with flowering vines cascading from one box to the next, or with zinnias for a pop of color next to their stark white shape. Of course, these planters don't have to live on the stairs—they'd also look great in rows on the edge of a patio or on shelves in a 3 × 3 grid. With good joints and plugs sanded flush to the surface, screw holes and seams disappear.

I made my planters from nominally 1-inch × 8-inch boards (actually ¾-inch × 7¼-inch), because the average rise, or height, of my stairs is 7½ inches. Choose the width of wood nearest to the rise of your stairs.

Each of these four wood planters takes about ten minutes to build, ten minutes to sand, and ten minutes to paint (although I can't necessarily guarantee a 30-minute project—time must be allotted for finding lost tools and picking unfortunate gnats out of wet paint).

MATERIALS

Three 1 in. × 8 in. × 6 ft. boards

One 1 in. × 10 in. × 4 ft. board

Two pieces of 1-in. scrap wood to be used for positioning (you will create these scraps when you are cutting pieces to length)

1¼-in. no. 8 deck screws

Weatherproof wood glue

Plugs

Paint or stain (optional)

TOOLS

Miter saw

Drill/driver

Quick-flip drive with a #8 ¹¹⁄₆₄-in. countersink bit

⅜-in. drill bit

Rubber mallet

Tape measure

Adjustable square

Painting or Staining the Boxes

Wet soil will cause the planters to degrade more quickly. To extend the life of the planters, paint or stain the inside and outside of the boxes with the least toxic water-resistant paint or stain you can find. Chemicals from paint can leach into soil, harming plants' health. If these planter boxes are meant for edible plants, I recommend not using paint or stain on the inside surface. The wood won't last as long, but you'll be able to feel good about what you're eating from your very own hand-built container garden.

 Cut the box wall pieces to length.

Using the miter saw, cut sixteen pieces from the 1 × 8s at 10½ in. long. If your miter saw can't cut the full width of the board, make one cut first, then, with the miter saw turned off, turn the board around, align the blade with the kerf (the space left from the first cut), and make the second cut.

2 **Construct the walls for the boxes.**

Arrange four wall pieces in a square so that each piece overlaps, and is overlapped by, one piece at the corners. Trace the end of each piece onto the face of its neighboring piece.

Measure and mark one side of each face piece for two screw holes.

Predrill for two counterbored holes on each face. Screw together the four box wall pieces. Repeat these steps for each box.

Cut the box bottoms to length. 3

Place a four-walled box assembly directly on the 1 × 10 board. (The 1 × 10 board, when centered inside the box, will leave about a ¼-in. gap on opposite sides for drainage.) Trace the two inside walls of the planter box form onto the 1 × 10 where it meets the box walls and cut the 1 × 10 to fit the inside of the box. Set the box bottom piece aside and repeat this step for the remaining three boxes.

4 Attach the box bottom.

Place two 1-in.-thick pieces of scrap wood, stacked, against the outside of the planter box and trace the top of the scrap stack onto the box. Remove the top scrap piece. Trace the top of the remaining scrap piece onto the planter box.

The two lines indicate where the box bottom will be positioned inside the box.

Using an adjustable square, mark two screw holes between these lines, 1½ in. in from either edge, and predrill two counterbored holes. Repeat the steps above on the opposite side of the box, for a total of four screw holes per box.

Place one piece of scrap wood inside the box form (it will sit on the work surface).

Place the box bottom inside the box form, on top of the scrap. Center the box bottom so there is about a ¼-in. gap on each side.

Screw the box walls to the box bottom.

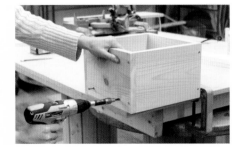

5 Drill drainage holes in the bottom of the box.

Remove the quick-flip drive and tighten a ⅜-in. drill bit in the drill/driver. Flip the box over and drill five or six holes in the bottom of the box for additional drainage.

Except for some worms, nobody will see these holes, so it doesn't matter if they are in a pretty arrangement.

Put a small drop of glue into each screw hole, insert a plug, and gently pound the plugs into the holes with a mallet. Sand the plugs so that they're flush with the surface of the wood. Sand the joints well for a seamless effect. Paint or stain the boxes, if you like.

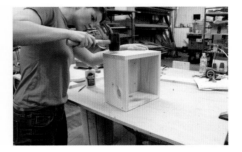

▲ The scrolled edge on the bottom of the flower box is for form and function: it's decorative and it allows air and water flow under the planter.

Flower Box

24 in. wide × 9½ in. deep × 7¼ in. high

The scrolled cut-out on the bottom of this flower box adds interest and allows air and water to flow underneath. Although it looks somewhat fancy, a scroll is one of the easiest shapes to make with a band saw or a scroll saw. As an added bonus, because it looks more complicated than, say, a rounded arch, even if the scroll is not cut perfectly symmetrically, it tricks the eye into thinking it is. Consequently, scrolls can be found on many historic styles of furniture.

The dimensions I've given can be changed to fit different-size plants or spaces as long as all of the box's side pieces are cut from boards of the same width.

If you are planning to attach this box to a wall or fence, make sure the object it is being attached to is structurally sound enough to hold the weight of the wood, soil, and plants when waterlogged.

MATERIALS

One 1 in. × 8 in. × 6 ft.

One scrap 1 in. × 8 in. × 30 ft.

1⅝-in. no. 8 deck screws

Weatherproof wood glue

Plugs

Paint or stain (optional; I used a clear water-based polyurethane stain with a satin gloss)

TOOLS

Miter saw

Adjustable square

Band saw, coping saw, scroll saw, or jigsaw

Clamp

Rubber mallet

Drill/driver

Quick-flip drive with a #8 ¹¹⁄₆₄-in. countersink bit

¼-in. drill bit for drainage holes

1 Cut the box sides to length.

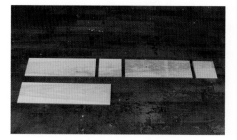

Using the miter saw, cut the 1 × 8 into two 24-in. pieces and two 8-in.-long pieces.

Ten-Inch Blades

If you are using a miter saw with a 10-in. blade, the cut will not go all the way through the width of the board. Flip the piece over and align it with the blade to complete the cut.

2 Mark and draw the scroll on the front face of one of the 24-in. pieces.

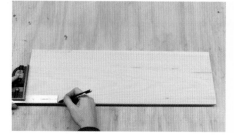

On the bottom of the face of one of the 24-in. pieces, use an adjustable square to measure 4 in. in from either side and mark both spots.

On the bottom of the face of this board, place the other 24-in. piece on its edge and trace its thickness onto the face of the first board.

This line indicates where the box bottom will end, so you'll never be making any cuts above this line.

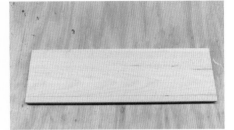

Find the center of the line that you've traced. Ensure it is the true center by measuring from both ends—you should have the same measurement from both ends.

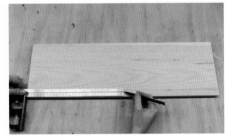

Draw one half of the scroll. It should begin at the 4-in. mark on the bottom edge of the piece, curve up to reach or almost reach the traced line, curve down to almost reach the bottom edge, and curve up to hit the center mark on the traced line. (If you like, practice on a piece of paper before drawing the scroll directly on the board.)

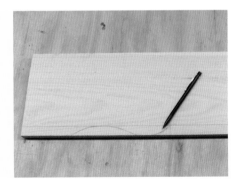

Cut the center line to the traced line. Since my 24-in.-long piece didn't fit that way through my band saw, I used a coping saw to cut the center line. Use a clamp or two to secure the board to the table while you cut it.

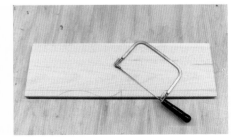

2 Cut the scroll. (Continued)

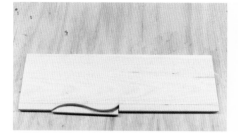

Using a band saw, jig saw, or coping saw, cut the first half of the scroll.

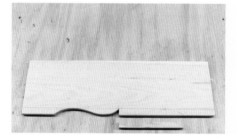

Flip the off-cut piece over and trace it on the other side.

Use a band saw, jig saw, or coping saw to cut the line you've just traced.

Using Paper to Trace the Scroll

If you had to recut your scroll and the off-cut isn't traceable, trace the new cut with a pencil onto paper and either cut the paper with scissors to trace, or flip the paper facedown on the board, align it with the center line and 4-in. line, and make a pencil rubbing.

Predrill the two 24-in. boards.

Trace a board's thickness onto both ends of the scrolled 24-in. board's face.

Mark three screw holes in the traced area and predrill for counterbored holes.

Trace a board's thickness onto the face of both ends of the other 24-in. board, mark for holes, and predrill.

4 Attach the 24-in. pieces to the 8-in. pieces.

Using a clamp as a cleat, stand one of the 8-in. pieces on its edge on the work surface. Using a drill/driver and 1⅝-in. screws, attach one of the 24-in. pieces to the 8-in. piece. Turn the project over and attach the other 8-in. piece to the assembly.

Place the assembly facedown on the work surface and align the other 24-in. piece with your fingers. Screw the other 24-in. piece into place.

Cut the box bottom to length and drill drainage holes. 5

Place the box on the bottom piece and trace its inside length.

Using a miter saw, cut the bottom board to length.

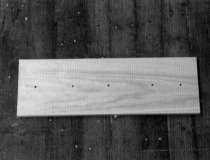

Drill a few ¼-in. drainage holes in the bottom piece. The pattern of the holes doesn't matter because it will be covered by soil. There will also be drainage on both sides of this bottom piece, so the holes should be roughly down the center of the box bottom's length.

6 Mark the location of the box bottom on the outside of the box's ends and predrill.

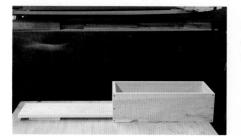

Place the box bottom on top of a piece of scrap wood next to an outside end of the box.

Trace the end of the box bottom on the outside end of the box.

Measure and mark for two holes in the area you've traced.

Predrill for counterbored holes and repeat on the other outside end of the box.

Place the box bottom on top of a piece of scrap wood (or two side-by-side pieces of scrap wood, if necessary).

Place the box assembly over the scrap piece and the box bottom, making sure the assembly is sitting on the work surface.

7 **Attach the box bottom.** (Continued)

The box bottom's edges should be centered, leaving a bit of space on both sides for drainage, and its ends should fit snugly inside the box.

Using the drill/driver and 1⅝-in. screws, attach the box to the box bottom.

Put a small drop of glue into each screw hole, insert a plug, and gently pound the plugs into the holes with a mallet. Sand the plugs so that they're flush with the surface of the wood. Paint or stain.

▲ The rope moulding gives the table nautical flair and is both decorative and functional: it keeps objects from rolling away. If you prefer a flat-surfaced table, but want to keep the nautical accent, wrap the rope moulding around the apron instead.

Nautical End Table

22½ in. × 22½ in. × 24 in. high

A quick project, this simple, stylish little table might make itself at home in the backyard of a beach cottage, ready to collect a tall pitcher of lemonade or a handful of seashells at the end of the day. The key to getting a perfect, sturdy table is to make sure all the screws have snugly joined the wood pieces together.

Optional rope moulding adds a nautical embellishment to the table's simple form; you can use any shape moulding, on the tabletop or around the apron, to personalize its look. If you attach the moulding around the apron, change the angle of the miter saw's blade (rather than the angle of its table, as in the instructions) to 45 degrees. For contrast, I gave the rope moulding a coat of clear polyurethane before attaching it. This table has light blue deck stain, but you could also try a deep red, a whitewash, or a navy blue for a similarly summery feel.

MATERIALS

Two 1 in. × 5 in. × 8 ft. boards

1⅝-in. screws

One 2 in. × 2 in. × 8 ft. board

One 1 in. × 2 in. × 8 ft. board

Weatherproof wood glue

Plugs

One 8 ft. length of ¾-in.-wide moulding (optional)

Eight 18 gauge ¾-in. brass brad nails (optional; for attaching the moulding)

Small hammer

Paint or stain (optional)

TOOLS

Miter saw

Drill/driver

Quick-flip drive with a #8 ¹¹⁄₆₄-in. countersink bit

Adjustable square

Clamps

Framing square

Rubber mallet

Sander

Small hammer

1 **Cut and construct the apron.**

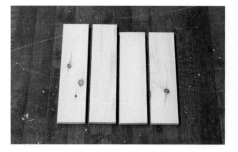

From one of the 1 × 5s, use the miter saw to cut two pieces at 18½ in. and two pieces at 17 in.

Trace the edge of another board on the ends of the 18½-in. pieces.

Mark for two screw holes at both ends of both 18½-in. pieces and predrill counterbored holes for the screws.

Set a cleat by positioning a clamp 17¾ in. from the corner of the work surface. Set one of the 17-in. pieces on its edge against the cleat, and place one of the 18½-in. pieces on its edge with the screw holes aligning with the 17-in. board. Using the drill/driver and 1⅝-in. screws, screw the boards together. Repeat until all four boards are screwed together in a square. Put a drop of glue into each hole, plug the holes, and sand (it's easier to sand the apron before the tabletop and legs are attached).

2 Cut and attach the tabletop pieces.

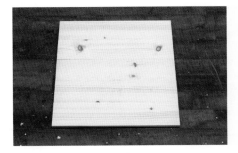

Cut five 1 × 5 pieces at 22½ in. Place the pieces face up on the work surface, abutting each other.

Place the apron on top of the tabletop pieces and use an adjustable square to center the apron at 2 in. in from all sides. Trace the inside and outside edges of the apron onto the tabletop pieces. Remove the apron and mark the three center tabletop pieces for four screw holes (two at each end, inside the lines you've traced), and mark the two outside pieces for three holes each (one in the middle and one on each end, inside the lines you've traced). Predrill for counterbored holes.

Place the tabletop boards on top of the apron and screw them in place.

Cut and attach the legs.

From the 2 × 2, cut four legs at 23¼ in.

Turn the tabletop over so the apron faces up. Place one leg in each of the inside corners of the apron. Mark the apron for two screw holes in the center of each leg. Clamp the leg in place. (The clamp may cover the top hole while you're screwing the bottom hole.)

3 Cut and attach the legs. (Continued)

Predrill the bottom hole for a counterbored hole and screw the leg in place using a 1⅝-in. screw.

Remove the clamp. With a framing square, check that the leg is square on both sides. Predrill the top hole for a counterbored hole and screw in place. Repeat with the three other legs.

4

Put a small drop of glue into each screw hole, insert a plug, and gently pound the plugs into the holes with a mallet. Sand the plugs so that they're flush with the surface of the wood. Paint or stain the table, if you like. If the moulding will cover the holes on the tabletop's surface, those holes don't need to be plugged.

5

Attach the moulding. (Optional)

Set the table of the miter saw to a 45-degree angle. Cut four pieces of moulding (as trapezoids, not parallelograms) at 18¼ in. at their longest. Paint or stain the rope moulding before attaching it to the tabletop. When the moulding is dry, glue and nail the moulding pieces to the tabletop. If you want to use different colors for the moulding and table, paint or stain the moulding and table before attaching the moulding.

A swing makes a welcoming garden even
more appealing.

Garden Swing

1¼ in. thick × 8 in. wide × 24 in. long

A child who grows up with a tree swing will forever have memories of their favorite tree. If you can, hang the swing on a live, robust, horizontal branch that is at least 8 inches in diameter with no obstructions to the flat ground below. If the tree is properly cared for, the tree and the people using the swing will develop a relationship with each other for the rest of their lives.

To avoid an awkward social situation involving a bruised backside, test the strength of your knots and the tree yourself before inviting someone else to try the swing. Regularly check the safety of the branch and swing.

The length of the swing is 24 inches. With luck, you won't have to buy a 12-foot board for this project: many hardware stores have short pieces, called off-cuts, or cull, that can be bought at a discount. These pieces are often cracked or warped, but you might find one that's not. Otherwise, buy a whole board and use the rest of it for other projects.

MATERIALS

One 2 in. × 8 in. × 24 in. board

Paint or stain (optional)

Rope with a diameter of at least ¾-in. (I used a rope with a diameter of ⅝ in.) The length should be four times the height of the tree branch, plus a few extra feet. Polyester and nylon are good rope materials that won't stretch. Check the label to see if it is meant to support human weight.

Heavy-duty scissors, or a knife that's strong enough to cut the rope

Lighter (for melting the ends of the rope)

TOOLS

Miter saw

Sander

Adjustable square

Drill press or drill/driver

Quick-flip drive with a #8 ¹¹⁄₆₄-in. countersink bit

¾-in. drill bit

1 Cut the wood to length and sand.

If your board is longer than 24 in., cut it to 24 in. Sand the piece on all six faces and all twelve corners to ensure sitting on it will be comfortable. I chamfered my corners, but you can round them over if you choose (see page 37).

2 Drill the holes for the rope and paint or stain the board.

Using an adjustable square, mark for four holes, 1½ in. in from the ends and sides.

Drill the holes using a ¾-in. drill bit. If you like, paint or stain the board, including the insides of the holes.

Tie the swing to the branch (or wherever you're hanging it). The following steps should be done on location. Cut two lengths of rope at twice the height of the limb, plus a few feet extra.

This first knot, the bowline (rhymes with stolen, not cow spine), will be thrown over the top of the limb. Make a loop about 2 ft. from the end of the rope. The end of the rope should be closest to you, and loop over the rest of the rope. Imagine the short end of the rope closest to you is a bunny. The loop is the bunny's hole, and the rest of the long rope on the other side of the loop is a tall tree next to her hole.

The bunny comes up and out of her hole.

Next, the bunny hops behind the tree.

Tie the swing to the branch. (Continued)

After spying a fox lurking nearby, the bunny quickly hops back into her hole. Phew! The bunny is safe.

There will be three lengths of rope below the knot (two forming a loop and one rope end) and one above. Pull on all three to tighten them.

Hold a lighter an inch below the rope ends until you see them start to melt.

When the rope ends are cool enough to touch, press the end strands together with your fingers. Repeat with the other length of rope.

Throw one rope over the tree branch.

Put the end of the rope through the loop.

3 **Tie the swing to the branch.** (Continued)

Pull the rope until the knot runs all the way up to the limb.

Give it a good tug until the knot tightens.

There should be a few feet of extra rope on the ground. Repeat with the other rope.

Thread the rope down through one of the holes in the swing.

Then thread it up through the hole on the opposite diagonal corner.

Thread the other rope through the remaining holes. The rope should make an X underneath the swing, and you should be holding the two rope ends. Tie one of the swing's sides in place temporarily so you can use both hands to tie half-hitches on the other.

3 **Tie the swing to the branch.** (Continued)

On the right side, loop one rope around the other about 4 in. above the swing's surface.

Pass the end of the rope below itself and pull tight.

Repeat this knot at least three times.

The finished knots will look like this. Repeat the three half-hitches on the other side of the swing. Make sure the swing seat is level. Sit on the swing to tighten all the knots.

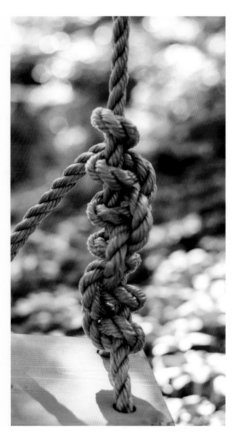

Cut the ends with heavy-duty scissors and melt them with a lighter. When the rope ends are cool enough to touch, press the end strands together with your fingers.

▲ The finished plant shelf with its grid of nine pots.
The pots seem to float through the shelves.

Plant Shelf

40 in. high × 42 in. wide × 5½ in. deep

Use this plant shelf indoors or outdoors for an herb library, decoration for a desolate part of a garden, or as a way to get more plants in a vertical space in that one sunny spot in your yard. If you live in a windy area, attach the shelf to a wall or deck with brackets for maximum outdoor wind-resistance.

I used a 3 × 3 grid for this plant shelf, but the concept can be adapted to a number of configurations: as a single shelf attached with brackets to a wall or under a window, or with holes sawn into the middle of a picnic table for a floral centerpiece. In any configuration, leave a minimum of 1 or 2 inches between the edges of the holes.

The pots should be tapered or have a lip at the top that will keep them from sliding through the holes. The size of the hole saw should fall between the diameter of the top of the pot and the bottom of the pot. Use any material that is suitable for the outdoors. The pots shown here are spray-painted terra-cotta against clear-coated wood. Galvanized metal pots on distressed black paint would feel industrial, or, for a cheerful look, paint the shelves white and paint each pot a different color of the rainbow.

MATERIALS

Three 1 in. × 6 in. × 6 ft. boards

1⅝-in. no. 8 deck screws

Weatherproof wood glue

Plugs

Paint or stain (optional)

Nine pots suitable for outdoor use (the pots used for this project are terra-cotta, 4¾ in. tall, with a 5¾-in. top diameter and a 3¼-in. bottom diameter)

TOOLS

Miter saw

Masking tape

Tape measure

Hole saw with an outside diameter that falls between the diameters of the top and bottom of the pot (the one I used for this project is 4¼ in.)

Drill press

Sander

Sandpaper

Adjustable square

Drill/driver

Quick-flip drive with a #8 ¹¹⁄₆₄-in. countersink bit

Clamp

Rubber mallet

1 Cut the pieces to length.

Using the miter saw, cut four 36-in. pieces—these will be for the sides and the two lower shelves of the unit. Cut one 42-in. piece—this will be the upper shelf. Use masking tape and a marker to label each piece.

2 Mark the shelves for holes.

Mark the two lower shelves at 6 in., 18 in., and 30 in. across their length and at the center of their width. Mark the top shelf at 9 in., 21 in., and 33 in. across its length and at the center of its width.

3 Set up the drill press to use the hole saw.

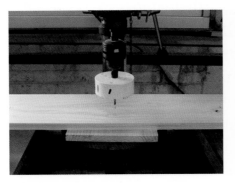

Hole saws usually come in a kit with multiple sizes. Determine which size you'll need for your flowerpots and screw the saw onto the mandrel. Position the table of the drill press so the hole saw's drill bit (the piece that sticks out of the center of the hole saw) goes through the hole in the center of the table.

Place a sacrificial board on the table of the drill press. Place the piece you are drilling on the sacrificial wood. Align the drill bit with one of the marks you made for holes and clamp the piece and the sacrificial board securely to the table. Turn the drill press on and slowly lower the drill bit. While you're drilling, the saw's teeth may fill up with sawdust. If they do, lift the lever, shut off the power, and use a pencil eraser to clear the sawdust. Then continue drilling.

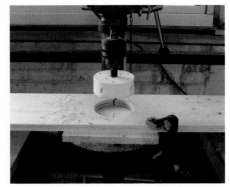

After drilling each hole, use a screwdriver or pencil eraser to push the wood out of the hole saw. Sand the edges of the holes.

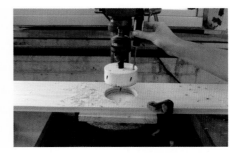

When you're finished, you'll have three holes in each of the two lower shelves and three holes in the top shelf.

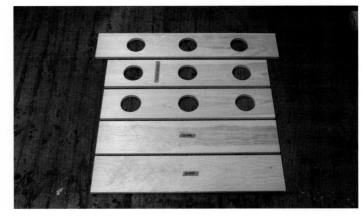

5 Mark the side pieces for screws and predrill.

Using a square, starting from the end of the side piece that will sit on the ground, mark both faces of the side pieces at 3 in. and 3¾ in., and also at 19½ in. and 20¼ in. These points indicate where the two lower shelves will be positioned. Mark two screw holes between the lines at 3 in. and 3¾ in. and two screw holes between the lines at 19½ in. and 20¼ in. and predrill for counterbored holes.

6 Attach the sides to the lower shelves.

Lay a side piece on its edge on a corner of the work surface. Attach a clamp to the work surface at the end of the shelf to provide something to push against when screwing. Attach the lowest shelf piece to the side piece.

Attach the other lower shelf piece to the side piece.

Attach the other side piece to the assembly.

Mark the top shelf for screws, predrill, and attach. 7

Place the top shelf on the floor. Stand the shelf assembly upside down on it and center it using an adjustable square.

Trace both faces of each side piece onto the top shelf. Mark the top shelf for screw holes.

Turn the assembly over, position the top shelf, predrill for screw holes, and attach the top shelf to the assembly.

8

Put a small drop of glue into each screw hole, insert a plug, and gently pound the plugs into the holes with a mallet. Sand the plugs so that they're flush with the surface of the wood. Paint or stain the wood if you like, let the paint dry, and insert the pots.

▲ A bench adds character to any garden, porch, or patio.

Two-Board Bench

18¾ in. high × 36 in. long × 7¼ in. wide

Clean, simple, and sturdy design with a minimum of waste: this concept sounds modern, but it's not—versions of this bench can be found in medieval, early-American colonial, and camp styles of furniture. Because of its simplicity, and the fact that it goes with any style of furniture and can be built in any size, it's one of my favorite projects in this book.

This bench is built from two 6-foot boards: one 1 × 8 and one 1 × 3. It can also be scaled down into a step stool using a 1 × 6 and a 1 × 3, with a 24-inch seat and legs that are 12 inches high. The bench can also be made longer and wider if you prefer. For a bench longer than 60 inches, add a third leg piece to the center, identical to the two outer legs.

MATERIALS

One 1 in. × 3 in. × 6 ft. board
One 1 in. × 8 in. × 6 ft. board
1⅝-in. no. 8 deck screws
Weatherproof wood glue
Plugs
Paint or stain (optional)

TOOLS

Miter saw
Band saw, jigsaw, or coping saw
Adjustable square
Drill/driver
Quick-flip drive with a #8 ¹¹⁄₆₄-in. countersink bit
Sander
Rubber mallet

1   Cut the boards to length.

Using the miter saw, cut the 1 × 3 into two 36 in. pieces. Cut the 1 × 8 into one 36 in. piece and two 18 in. pieces for the legs.

2   Cut the legs to shape.

On one of the 18-in. pieces, draw a notch for the shape of the legs. The notch can be any shape you like: the one used for this bench is a triangle, but you could make a rounded arch, a peaked arch, or a scroll shape. Leave at least 2 in. on either side of the notch for the feet, and don't let the peak of the notch go above 12 in. from the bottom of the legs. The legs on this bench have 3-in.-wide feet on either side of the notch, and the peak of the notch is 8 in. from the bottom.

Using a band saw, jigsaw, or coping saw, cut the notch in the first leg piece. Place the notched leg onto the uncut leg piece and trace the notch onto the uncut leg piece. Cut out the notch on the second leg.

Trace the end of a 36-in. side support onto the upper corners of the leg pieces. Cut these pieces out carefully, starting by cutting just inside the lines, test fitting the 1 × 3 board in the cutout, and expanding the cut as necessary.

Cut the side supports to shape.

3

Turn the table of the miter saw until it is at 45 degrees.

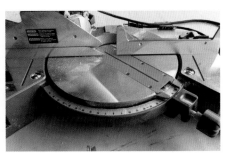

3 **Cut the side supports to shape.** (Continued)

Cut both ends of the two 36-in. side support pieces at 45 degrees. Each end of the cut should be facing opposite directions—the side supports should be shaped like a trapezoid, not a parallelogram. If the side supports turn out to be slightly shorter than 36 in., don't worry. Just cut both side supports to the same length and then cut the length of the 1 × 8 seat piece to the same length.

4 **Predrill the side supports.**

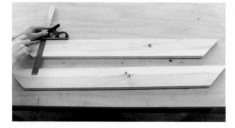

Using a square, draw a line from the bottom of the obtuse angle at both ends of the side support pieces. Draw another line ¾ in. in from this line. The screw holes should be positioned inside the two lines you've drawn.

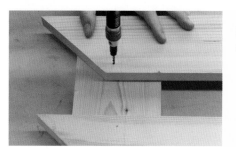

Mark for screw holes and predrill for counterbored holes.

Attach the side supports to the legs. 5

Place the legs on their edges on the work surface. Place one side support in the corner space you cut for it in step 2 and use a square to ensure that the legs and the side support are at 90 degrees. Use 1⅝-in. screws to attach the two side supports to the legs, checking for square after every screw.

Attach the bench top to the leg assembly. 6

Place the bench top face up on the work surface. Place the leg assembly on top of it and trace around the leg assembly and on the outside of the legs.

6 **Attach the bench top to the leg assembly.** (Continued)

Set aside the leg assembly and turn the bench top over. Inside the lines you've traced, mark and predrill for five counterbored holes along both seat supports and one screw hole in the center of each leg.

Screw the bench top to the leg assembly.

Put a small drop of glue into each screw hole, insert a plug, and gently pound the plugs into the holes with a mallet. Sand the plugs so that they're flush with the surface of the wood. Paint or stain.

▲ The finished chickadee house. The birdhouse's floor is removable so that
the house can be cleaned out between nesting seasons (see page 2).

Gothic Arch Chickadee House

6½ in. long × 6½ in. wide × 7⅔ in. high

This little house is designed for chickadees, although you might find nuthatches, titmice, or wrens making their home in your creation. Chickadees are one of the most abundant and fun birds to watch and, with patience, can even be trained to eat out of your hands.

The form for the roof was inspired by the peaked-arch windows of Carpenter Gothic architecture—a style not of soaring European cathedrals, but of simple rural American homes and churches popular in the nineteenth century.

The roof is made from furring strips—small scraps of leftover wood—and the walls are attached with counterbored and plugged holes, but the floor is attached with screws that are flush with the wood's surface so it can be removed to clean out nests.

Chickadees may stay in their houses year-round, even in climates that get very hot in the summer and below freezing in the winter. If you choose to paint your house, paint the roof a neutral color so that it doesn't get too hot in summer. Chickadees like their houses in shady locations, 5 to 15 feet off the ground, facing away from the wind. I screwed two hooks into the top and bottom of the back of mine to attach it to a tree.

MATERIALS

One 1 in. × 4 in. × 13 in. board

Two 1 in. × 8 in. × 8 in. wood scraps

1¼-in. no. 8 deck screws

Weatherproof wood glue

Plugs

Approximately twelve ¾ in. × ⅛ in. furring strips (cut from a total of about 10 ft.)

Paint or stain (optional)

Small ¾-in. brad nails

Two cup hooks (optional; for hanging on a tree)

Two eyehooks (optional; for hanging on a tree)

TOOLS

Miter saw

Drill/driver

Quick-flip drive with a #8 ¹¹⁄₆₄-in. countersink bit

Adjustable square

Tape measure

Band saw, scroll saw, or coping saw

Sander

1⅛-in. drill bit or hole saw

Rubber mallet

Clamp

Sandpaper

Small drill bit the same diameter as the nails

Small hammer

121

1   Construct the side walls and floor.

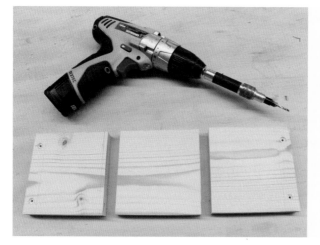

Cut the 1 × 4 into three 3½-in. squares. Mark two screw holes on two of the squares, and predrill for flush screws (do not counterbore these holes). These are the sides of the birdhouse, and the piece without any screw holes is the floor.

Attach the walls to the floor, making a U shape. Screw through the walls into the floor.

2   Cut the front and back arch-shaped walls.

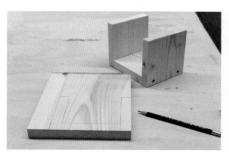

Trace the U-shaped assembly on one of the 1 × 8 scraps.

Mark the spot where you'd like the roof's peak to be, centering it with an adjustable square or tape measure. Draw an arc from the outside edge of one of the birdhouse's walls to the peak.

Using a band saw, scroll saw, jigsaw, or coping saw, cut along the line you've drawn.

Use the off-cut piece to trace the arch shape onto the other side of the wood.

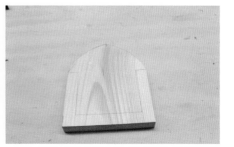

Cut along that line to create the arched front wall.

2 Cut the front and back arch-shaped walls. (Continued)

Trace the arched front wall onto the other 1 × 8 scrap. Cut the shape out to create the arched back wall.

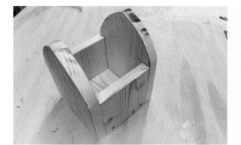

Holding the two arched walls face to face, sand the edges. They should fit flush with the outer edges of the square walls.

3 Attach the arch-shaped walls to the side walls.

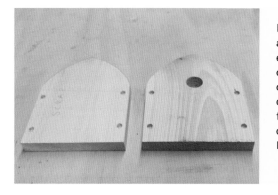

Find the vertical center of one of the arch-shaped walls. Drill a hole for the entryway in the center with a 1⅛-in. drill bit or hole saw. The hole doesn't have to be centered from top to bottom—it can be closer to the top, as it is in this project. Mark four holes on each arch-shaped wall for drilling to the side walls (not the floor). Predrill for counterbored holes.

Screw the arch-shaped walls into the side walls. Put a small drop of glue into each screw hole on the front and back, insert a plug, and gently pound the plugs into the holes with a mallet. Sand the plugs so that they're flush with the surface of the wood.

Sand the assembly.

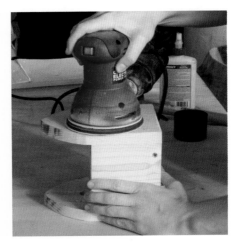

Cut the roof pieces. 4

The roof pieces will be flush with the birdhouse's back wall and overhanging the front wall by ½ in. From the furring piece, cut roof pieces at 6½ in. long. This chickadee house uses twelve roof pieces, but the number of roof pieces that you need will depend on the arc of your roof. To determine how many pieces you'll need, lay the house on its back on the work surface. Starting at the peak, place roof pieces along its roofline until there are enough to make a roof from side wall to side wall.

5 Optional: Angle the edges of the two topmost roof pieces to make a tight seam.

This step will add about a half hour to the project. Have extra roof pieces on hand if you need to start over. If you don't want to do this step, move ahead to step 6.

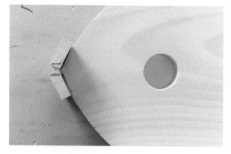

Lay the birdhouse assembly on the work surface, with the wall with the hole in it facing up. Position the two topmost roof pieces at the peak of the roof and, from the top corners of the roof pieces, draw two lines straight down. The lines should be parallel to each other.

Clamp a sheet of sandpaper to the table. Holding one of the marked roof pieces with two hands, sand one of the long corners of the piece to make an angled edge. Do the same with the other roof piece, checking them against each other often to make sure they'll meet in a seam.

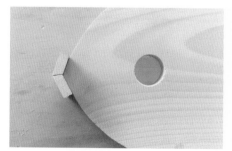

Once you've sanded them sufficiently, they'll meet in a tight seam at the top of the birdhouse.

Paint or stain the birdhouse. 6

If you would like the house to be a different color from the roof, paint or stain it now (I waited until after putting the roof on, but it would have taken much less time to do it before). Do not paint or stain the inside of the house.

Predrill holes for the roof pieces. 7

Lay the house on its back on the work surface. Position one rooftop piece on the roof and trace where the edges of the front and back walls will abut the rooftop piece.

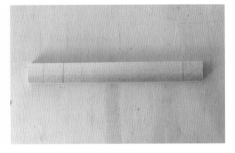

You should have three lines traced on the roof piece: two for both edges of the front wall and one for the front edge of the back wall. (The back of the roof pieces and the back wall will be flush with each other, so you don't need to trace a line along the back edge of the back wall.)

Arrange all roof pieces side-by-side. Use an adjustable square to continue the lines you drew on the first roof piece across all the roof pieces.

7 **Predrill holes for the roof pieces.** (Continued)

Using a sacrificial board to avoid drilling holes in the work surface, predrill the roof pieces with a small bit, the same size as the nails. Position one hole in between the two lines you drew at the front of the roof piece and one hole between the line and the back edge of the roof piece. Predrilling the holes will prevent cracks in the wood from the nails. There should be two holes in each piece.

8 **Attach the roof pieces.**

Starting with one of the topmost roof pieces (one of the pieces you sanded, if you chose to do that), place a dab of glue over each predrilled hole on the inside face.

Gently nail the piece to the arched walls.

Continue nailing the abutting roof pieces until the entire roof is covered.

Hang the birdhouse on a tree. (Optional) **9**

Cup hooks and eyehooks hold the top and bottom of the house to the tree trunk. Turn both hooks to the side, slide the house on, and turn the top hook up and the bottom hook down.

▲ The finished potting bench, ready to be put to work. The tabletop is stained with gray and the legs are painted with black enamel paint. The space between each tabletop board was created using a dowel as a spacer instead of measuring the distance between each board—this method saves time and is more accurate.

Potting Bench

60 in. long × about 40 in. wide × 34¾ in. high

A quick-and-easy project to make, this potting bench looks industrial-chic and is sturdy enough to hold heavy pots and soil. The tabletop boards have spaces between them to let rain, snow, and dirt fall through. In order to accommodate the depth of the pots you might be working with, the height of the table is between dining table and work surface height. If you'd like to make this a dining table, change the height of the leg pipes to 29 inches.

The pipes and fittings I used were reclaimed from an old factory building. If you are using found pipes, make sure the threads are usable before you start this project. If you are purchasing new pipes, you have the luxury of choosing which fittings you like best. Not all fittings require threads, so if your pipe is not threaded, use clamps instead of threaded fittings.

Unless you can buy pipes already cut to your specifications, you'll need a pipe cutter. A manual pipe cutter resembles a C-clamp with a cutting wheel, and they make a clean cut by being hand-rotated around the pipe. They're inexpensive and can be purchased at hardware stores.

MATERIALS

Four 14-in. lengths of ¾-in. black pipe, threaded at one end

Four 34-in. lengths of ¾-in. black pipe, threaded at one end

One 48-in. length of ¾-in. black pipe, threaded at both ends

Anti-rust spray enamel

Two 3-way threaded pipe connectors

Four floor flanges

Four T-clamps

One 1 in. × 4 in. × 8 ft. board

Five 1 in. × 4 in. × 6 ft. boards

1⅝-in. no. 8 deck screws

Two 1 in. × 5 in. × 6 ft. boards

One 1 in. × 8 in. × 6 ft. board

Two 1 in. × 10 in. × 6 ft. boards

Sixteen ¾-in. outdoor screws, to attach the floor flanges to the underside of the tabletop

Weatherproof wood glue

Plugs

(Continued on next page)

For the tabletop I used boards with different widths that I found in a pile of discounted scrap lumber at my local hardware store (in the photos you can see that the tabletop boards are slightly warped). Use straight boards for the apron to ensure the structure has all 90-degree angles. No matter the size of each tabletop board, the total of the widths of boards should be equal or greater than the width of the apron.

If you plan to put more than 200 pounds on your tabletop (bags of potting soil can be heavy), cut two additional 1 × 4 support boards for the apron at 35 inches and make the legs ¾ inch shorter.

TOOLS

Pipe cutter

Painter's tape

Abrasive cleaning pad

Adjustable wrench

Miter saw

Drill/driver

Quick-flip drive with a #8 $^{11}\!/_{64}$-in. countersink bit

Two 48-in. dowel spacers with a $^5\!/_{16}$-in. diameter

Speed square

Ruler

$^{11}\!/_{64}$-in. drill bit

Rubber mallet

Safety Note

Be careful when handling pipe—it's heavy. When the pipes are on your work surface, put clamps on the edges of the work surface to prevent the pipes from rolling off.

Cut the pipes to length. 1

To cut pipe using a pipe cutter, measure and mark where you want to cut the pipe, and snugly tighten the pipe cutter on the mark. Spin the pipe cutter around the pipe, and tighten the knob a small amount every turn or two until the pipe is cut. Cut four 14-in. lengths, threaded at one end, for the horizontal supports and four 34-in. lengths, threaded at one end, for the legs.

Spray the first coat of enamel on the pipes. 2

Tape the threaded parts of the pipes, including the threads of the 48-in.-long pipe. Rub the pipes with an abrasive cleaning pad to roughen up the surface so the paint sticks. Spray all sides of the pipes. You'll apply a second coat in step 3, after the structure is assembled.

Assemble the center pipe structure. 3

Assemble the center structure, which is shaped like a capital I. Using the two 3-way pipe connectors, attach the 48-in. center support piece to the four 14-in. horizontal support pieces. Attach the floor flanges to the leg pipes and stand them up. (The floor flanges will eventually be attached to the underside of the table, so they will be upside down in the final assembly.)

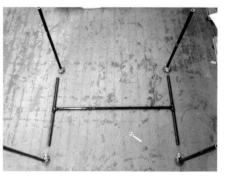

Assemble the center pipe structure. (Continued)

Attach the capital I–shaped structure to the legs using the T-clamps. Use a chair or another object at a workable height to balance the I-shaped structure while you're attaching the legs. Adjust the fittings until all angles are right angles. Spray a second coat of enamel on the pipes, including the fittings.

4

Construct the table apron.

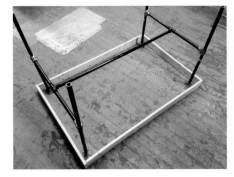

From the 1 × 4 × 8 ft. board, cut two pieces at 37 ¼ in. These are the apron ends. From the 1 × 4 × 6 ft. boards, cut two pieces at 53 ¼ in., and one piece at 35 ¾ in. These are the apron sides and the support piece. Arrange the apron boards on the floor around the leg structure to make sure the flanges fit nicely inside the corners with room to spare.

Measure and mark for two screw holes at each end of the end pieces, predrill for counterbored holes, and screw the end pieces to the side pieces with 1⅝-in. screws. Mark a vertical line at the center of the outer face of each side piece. Counterbore for two holes on each side piece and attach them to the 35¾-in. support piece.

Arrange and center the tabletop boards on the table apron. **5**

Move the apron to the work surface. Arrange the tabletop boards on the apron in any order that is pleasing to you, as long as the narrowest pieces, the 1 × 4s, are not the outside pieces. Use the 48-in. dowel spacers (one at each end) with a 5⁄16-in. diameter to space the boards evenly apart. I arranged the tabletop boards as follows:

Piece 1: 1 × 10

Piece 2: 1 × 5

Piece 3: 1 × 4

Piece 4: 1 × 10

Piece 5: 1 × 4

Piece 6: 1 × 5

Piece 7: 1 × 8

Label the position of each board with masking tape.

On both long sides of the tabletop, there will be a 2¾-in. overhang on either side of the apron. Set a speed square to 2¾ in. and measure on both sides once you're done placing your boards.

To ensure the tabletop will be centered on the apron, add the widths of all the boards to the widths of all the spaces between them. Subtract the width of your apron from that, and divide by two. This will be the distance the outermost boards hang over the apron on either side. [(Total width of boards) + (Total width of spaces) − (width of apron)] / 2 = distance from outside of apron to outside of tabletop.]

6 Mark and screw the tabletop boards to the apron.

With the ruler, measure the first board again to make sure it is placed correctly, 5½ in. from the end of the board to the outside of the apron. Measure and mark where the board sits on the table apron. Mark for four screws, predrill for counterbored holes, and screw the board to the apron with 1⅝-in. screws.

7 Attach the remaining tabletop boards.

Now that the first board is attached, use the dowel spacers and the speed square to align the next board. Mark, predrill for counterbored holes, and screw with 1⅝-in. screws.

Repeat until all the boards are attached.

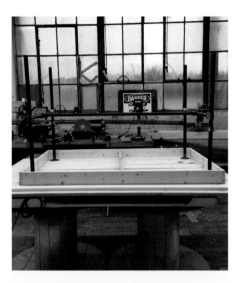

Turn the tabletop upside down on the work surface. Center the leg structure on the underside of the tabletop.

Predrill the holes (not for counter-bored holes) with the $^{11}/_{16}$-in. drill bit, making sure the predrilled holes don't go all the way through the tabletop, and screw the legs in place with ¾-in. screws.

Additional Support

If you are planning on putting more than 200 pounds on the potting bench, cut two additional 1 × 4 boards at 35 in. and attach them to the underside of the tabletop where the legs will be attached. Screw the flanges through the support board onto the underside of the tabletop with 1½-in. screws. The support boards will provide extra shear strength.

9

Put a small drop of glue into each screw hole, insert a plug, and gently pound the plugs into the holes with a mallet. Sand the plugs so that they're flush with the surface of the wood. Paint or stain.

▲ A rolling coffee table works nicely on a patio, where it can be moved to any location you like—sunny or shady. Casters make the table mobile and keep it off the ground.

Rolling Coffee Table

35½ in. long × 20 in. wide × 17 in. high

The brown stain and white paint on this rolling coffee table reminds me of a cappuccino—a drink that can be enjoyed with scones from atop this table on an early autumn morning.

I used casters because this table is meant for use on a patio, but it would also look great with tapered legs like the ones in the Slat Bench project. It can also be scaled down, without the support pieces, to the size of an end table. There are four support pieces inside the table, and the casters are attached, with bolts, to two of the support pieces through the bottom boards of the table. I gave the support pieces angled ends because I like the way the angles look, but you can opt to not angle the ends.

MATERIALS

Paint (I used white paint)

Stain (I used brown stain)

Three 1 in. × 5 in. × 8 ft. boards

One 1 in. × 3 in. × 8 ft. board

Two 1 in. × 4 in. × 8 ft. boards

Masking tape (optional; to label the boards)

One 48-in. dowel with a ⅜-in. diameter

1¼-in. no. 8 deck screws

Four 6-in. swivel casters with a flat, square top plate

Sixteen ¼-in. diameter, thread × 2-in. long bolts

Sixteen ¼-in. diameter nuts

Thirty-two ¼-in. washers (these washers are nominally ¼-in. but have an inside diameter of ⁵⁄₁₆-in. to allow you to easily slip the washer on the bolt)

1⅝-in. no. 8 deck screws

Weatherproof wood glue

Plugs

(Continued on next page)

◀ The four support pieces have angled ends. The casters are bolted to the support boards from underneath the table.

TOOLS

Miter saw

Framing square

Drill/driver

Quick-flip drive with a #8 $^{11}/_{64}$-in. countersink bit

$^{3}/_{8}$-in. drill bit

Two wrenches, adjustable or ¼ in.

Rubber mallet

1 Paint or stain the boards.

Trying to paint between the boards after the table has been constructed is a headache, especially if you plan to use alternating colors, so apply the first coat or two of paint (or stain) to the boards before they've been cut. Save the rest of the paint (or stain) for touch-ups after the table has been constructed.

2 Cut the support pieces.

Using the miter saw, cut four pieces from a 1 × 5 at 18 in. If you'd like angled support pieces, like the ones shown above, cut angles at both ends of each support board at 22½ degrees. The edges of the support pieces should form a trapezoid, not a parallelogram. Set the saw back to 90 degrees. Set the support pieces aside until step 4.

Cut the remaining pieces to length. 3

Set a stop on the miter saw at 12 in. Cut two pieces from each remaining board (the 1 × 3, the 1 × 4s, and the 1 × 5s) at 12 in. Set another stop at 35½ in. and cut two pieces from each remaining board at 35½ in. You will now have twenty pieces, ten at 12 in. and 10 at 35½ in.

Arrange the four 1 × 4 pieces on the floor end to end, starting with a 12-in. piece, then a 35½-in. piece, then a 12-in. piece, and then a 35½-in. piece. Next to the 1 × 4 pieces, arrange the four 1 × 5 pieces, also starting with a 12-in. piece, followed by a 35½-in. piece, and so on, and then arrange the 1 × 3s, then the 1 × 5s, and finally the remaining 1 × 4s.

If you like, label the pieces A, B, C, D, and E to help keep them organized as you work through the next few steps.

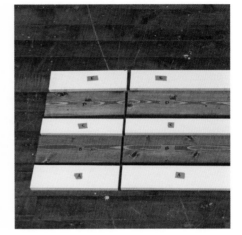

Attach the upper support pieces to the underside of the tabletop pieces. 4

Using a framing square, place all five 35½-in. tabletop pieces in order, facedown on the work surface. Use the spacer dowel to space them evenly apart. Trace a line ¾ in. (the thickness of the side boards) from both ends of the tabletop pieces. This line marks where the outer edge of the side pieces will be positioned. Place a support piece, with its ends angled toward the underside of the tabletop, with its edge on this line. (The edges should not be flush with the ends of the tabletop pieces.) It should be centered between the two outermost edges of the tabletop, about $^{15}/_{16}$ in. from either edge. Position the other support piece at the other end of the underside of the table.

4 **Attach the upper support pieces to the underside of the tabletop pieces.** (Continued)

On both support pieces, mark and predrill for counterbored holes so that three screws enter each tabletop piece in a triangular formation.

Screw both supports to the first tabletop piece using 1¼-in screws. Place the spacer between the first tabletop piece and the second, and screw both support pieces to the second tabletop piece, and so on, until all five tabletop pieces are attached to the upper support pieces.

5 **Attach the lower supports to the top side of the table bottom.**

Using the framing square, place the five pieces for the bottom of the table in order, face up. As you did in step 4, space the pieces apart using the spacer dowel and trace a line the thickness of the side pieces at both ends of the table bottom pieces. Place the support piece, with its ends angled toward the table bottom, with its edge on this line. (The edges should not be directly on the ends of the tabletop pieces.)

The support piece should be centered between the two outermost edges of the tabletop, about $^{15}/_{16}$ in. in from either edge.

On both support pieces, predrill holes so three screws will enter each tabletop piece through the support pieces.

Place the casters on the support pieces on the bottom of the table, centered about ¾ in. from each end, and trace the holes where the bolts will go. Then attach the support to the table bottom pieces with 1¼-in. screws, one by one with the spacer dowel. Make sure you are not putting a screw where the piece will be drilled through for the casters. (If a hole for a caster aligns with a pre-drilled hole, predrill a new screw hole.)

With a piece of scrap wood underneath where you will be drilling, drill the holes for the bolts with a ⅜-in. drill bit (you won't attach the casters until later).

6 **Attach the side pieces to the support pieces on the table bottom.**

Trace a line ¾-in. from either end of all the side pieces. Predrill the face of each side piece for counterbored holes. To ensure the screws enter the support pieces (and not thin air), do not drill holes in the outermost corners of the four outermost side pieces, the 1 × 4 × 12s. Instead, the outermost holes in these four pieces should be on the vertical center line. Using 1⅝-in. screws, attach the side pieces to the support piece on the table bottom assembly. You won't need to use the spacer dowel, because the table bottom assembly has already been properly spaced.

Attach the remaining side boards to the support boards on the other end.

Attach the tabletop. **7**

Screw the upper end of the side pieces to the support pieces on the tabletop assembly.

Attach the casters. **8**

Place the table on its side and, using two wrenches (one for the bolt and one for the nut), attach the casters using two washers for each bolt.

9

Put a small drop of glue into each screw hole, insert a plug, and gently pound the plugs into the holes with a mallet. Sand the plugs so that they're flush with the surface of the wood. Touch-up all the unpainted (or unstained) parts of the table.

▲ A slat bench adds a touch of midcentury-modern
  sophistication to any patio or yard.

Slat Bench

49½ in. long × 18 in. wide × 14 in. high

Slat benches are landmarks of midcentury-modern design, and their popularity continues today. Inspired by George Nelson's 1946 platform bench and Harry Bertoia's 1952 Bertoia Bench, this one has a similar clean-lined design but a much simpler construction.

Purchasing legs that screw on to mounting hardware saves the work of building the legs yourself, and screwing the slats to the end pieces rather than making complicated joinery makes this bench an easy and sturdy project for beginners.

Every piece of this bench is supported by every other piece: the outer and inner slats connect to the support pieces, which connect to the legs. I painted the legs black, but they would also look terrific with the top of the legs the same color as the bench and the bottoms of the legs dipped in white or gold paint.

MATERIALS

Stain

Five 1 in. × 2 in. × 8 ft. boards

Two 1 in. × 3 in. × 8 ft. boards

1⅝-in. screws

Four 12-in. legs with mounting hardware (I used Waddell Manufacturing Round Taper legs and angled top plates)

Weatherproof wood glue

Plugs

TOOLS

Sander

Speed square

Miter saw

¾-in.-thick spacer

Clamp

Drill/driver

Quick-flip drive with a #8 ¹¹⁄₆₄-in. countersink bit

Rubber mallet

Apply the first coat of stain.

In order to avoid having to apply stain in between the slats of the finished bench, sand and apply the first coat of stain to all seven boards before cutting them. (After the bench is assembled, you'll need to do more sanding and touch-up staining.)

2 Cut all the pieces to length.

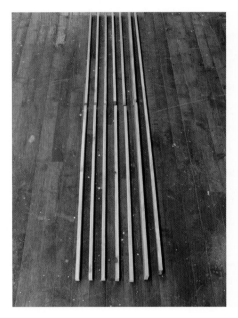

On the work surface, set a stop at 48 in. from the blade of the miter saw. Cut all five 1 × 2s and one 1 × 3 into 48-in. pieces. You'll have ten 1 × 2 × 48-in. pieces for the middle slats and two 1 × 3 × 48-in. pieces for the two side slats.

Cut the remaining 1 × 3 into two 18-in. pieces for the end pieces and two 16½-in. pieces for the support pieces underneath the slats.

Mark and predrill the end pieces. 3

Place the two 18-in. end pieces on the work surface. Use the edge of one end piece to mark vertical lines ¾ in. in from both ends of the board. Then do the same on the other end piece.

The two rectangles represent where you will predrill counterbored holes for the two outer-most boards (the two 1 × 3 × 48-in. boards).

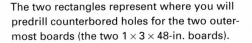

Place one of the 1 × 2 slat pieces on an 18-in. end piece with its bottom edge aligned with the end piece's bottom edge. The lines you traced in the previous step should be facing up. From one of the lines you traced in the previous step to the other, trace the slat onto the face of the 18-in. end piece.

The 18-in. end piece should look like this.

SLAT BENCH

3

Mark and predrill the end pieces. (Continued)

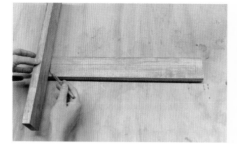

Align the edge of a ¾-in.-thick board with one of the vertical lines you have drawn on the 18-in. end piece. Trace a line along the edge.

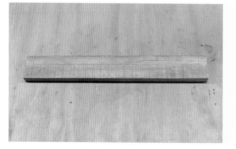

Continue tracing all the way across the board, until there are 22 evenly spaced vertical lines. The spaces represent the spaces where 2-in.-wide slats will be positioned and the spaces between the 2-in.-wide slats.

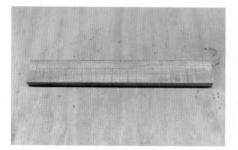

Mark for two screw holes in both of the two outermost sections of the board.

Mark for two screw holes on each of the ten sections where the 2-in.-wide slats will sit. You should have marks for screw holes in every other section; do not mark the spaces in between.

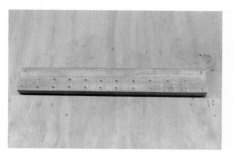

Predrill all the holes for counterbored holes and repeat the process with the other end piece.

Arrange the pieces on the work surface. **4**

Place one of the end pieces on the end of the work surface with the predrilled holes facing out. Using a speed square, place the two outermost (1 × 3 × 48-in.) pieces at right angles to the end piece. Position the ten 2-in.-wide slats between the two end pieces (when you screw them together, you'll be using a spacer to get the measurements exactly right). Clamp a board at the other end of the slats, so you'll have something to push against when you're screwing the pieces together.

Screw the end pieces to the slats. **5**

Screw the two 1 × 3 × 48-in. outermost slats to one end piece. Push the slats against the board clamped to the table. Place a ¾-in.-thick spacer between one of the outermost slats and the 2-in.-wide slat next to it. Screw the end piece to the 2-in.-wide slat.

Continue using the spacer as you're attaching the end piece to all the slats. Turn the assembly around and attach the other end piece in the same manner.

6 Attach support pieces.

Place the 16½-in. support pieces 7 in. from either end, predrill one hole per slat, and screw in place.

Mark and predrill two screws on the outermost slats at both ends of the support pieces.

Attach the mounting hardware and legs. **7**

On the support pieces, measure and mark 1½ in. in from the outside of the bench and attach two top plates to each support piece. If you're using angled top plates, as I did, be sure the angles are all facing outward.

Screw the legs in place.

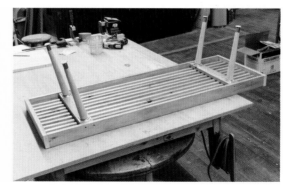

Put a small drop of glue into each screw hole, insert a plug, and gently pound the plugs into the holes with a mallet. Sand the plugs so that they're flush with the surface of the wood. Touch up the stain. **8**

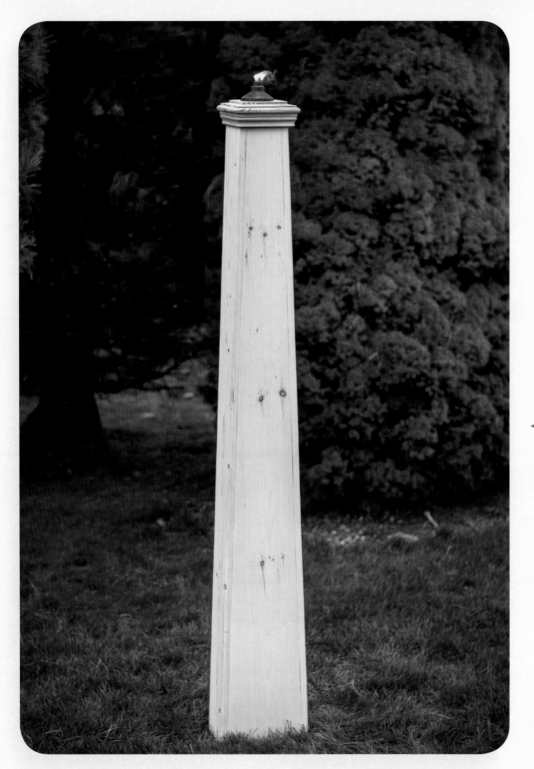

◀ The torchiere has two rectangular sides and two trapezoidal sides.

Torchiere

10½ in. wide × 5⅜ in. thick × 73½ in. high

At 6 feet high, this trapezoidal column with a flame shooting from the top makes an imposing impression. Torchieres add ambience to summertime evening gatherings: build a few and scatter them throughout the garden, position a few around the perimeter of your patio, or put two at the beginning of a walkway for grand entrance. Whatever you decide to do with this torchiere, it's sure to make a statement.

By itself, this torchiere doesn't balance well in wind, so it is designed with an inner structure to hold stakes that can be inserted in the ground. I used galvanized pipe because I had some at my shop; you can also use PVC pipe or wooden dowels with sharpened ends.

To evoke the sandstone columns of an ancient era, I used a sand-colored deck stain on the wood. It would also be fun to paint patterns on this torchiere.

MATERIALS

Fence-post cap with a flat top, for a nominally 6 × 6 post (I used a post cap made of pressure-treated wood; if you do be sure to wear a mask)

Two 1 in. × 10 in. × 6 ft. boards

One 1 in. × 2 in. × 4 ft. board

1⅝-in. no. 8 deck screws

Two 24-in.-long stakes with an ¹¹⁄₁₆-in. diameter

One 1 in. × 5 in. × 2 ft. board

Two 1 in. × 5 in. × 6 ft. boards

Weatherproof wood glue

Plugs

Paint or stain (optional)

Tiki torch fuel-replacement canister with a metal lid

TOOLS

3-in. hole saw

Drill press

Circular saw

Miter saw

Pipe cutter, if your stakes are metal

Drill/driver

Quick-flip drive with a #8 ¹¹⁄₆₄-in. countersink bit

Clamp

Sander

Rubber mallet

1   **Cut the hole in the fence-post cap for the fuel canister.**

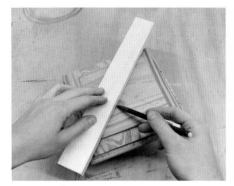

To find the center of the fence post cap, mark an X from corner to corner.

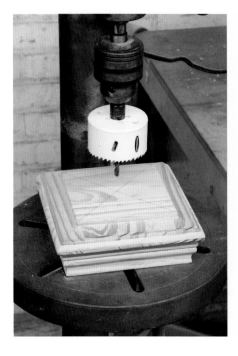

Chuck a 3-in. hole saw in the drill press. Position the table of the drill press so the hole saw's drill bit is aligned with the hole in the center of the table. Align the drill bit with the center of the X you made. Turn the drill press on and slowly lower the drill bit. Drill slowly.

While you're drilling the saw's teeth might fill up with sawdust. If they do, lift the lever, shut off the power, and use a pencil eraser to clear the sawdust. Then continue drilling until the hole is completely drilled.

Mark and cut the two trapezoid front and back pieces. **2**

At the end of one of the 1 × 10s, measure and mark 3¼ in. in from one side. Using another board, draw a diagonal line from this mark to the bottom corner of the board on the same side. Repeat with the other side to form the outline of a trapezoid.

Using a circular saw, cut along the lines you've drawn. Repeat the process with the other 1 × 10.

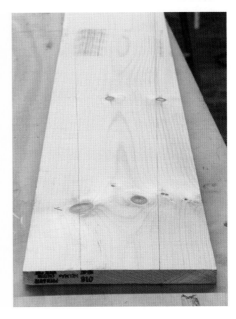

Make the stake sleeves. **3**

From the 1 × 2, cut four 12-in. lengths.

3 Make the stake sleeves. (Continued)

Center a 12-in. piece on its edge with one end flush with the bottom of one of the trapezoidal side pieces and trace both sides.

Place two 12-in. lengths on either side of the traced lines. Make sure the 24-in. stake will fit in between them.

Predrill for three holes and, using 1¼-in. screws, screw the two 12-in. pieces to the trapezoidal side piece. Repeat with the other trapezoidal side piece.

From the 1 × 5 × 2 ft. board, cut two 12-in. pieces. Predrill for two counter-bored holes and screw them over the two 1 × 2s on each trapezoidal piece. Make sure the stake fits inside the sleeve you've just made.

Attach the rectangular side pieces to the trapezoidal side pieces.

On the 1 × 5 × 6 ft. side pieces, measure and mark for a screw hole every foot along both sides of the face. Predrill the 1 × 5 rectangular side pieces.

Clamp one of the trapezoidal side pieces to the work surface, ¾-in. from the edge. Place the 1 × 5 rectangular side piece on its edge, with the predrilled holes facing out, and, using 1⅝-in.screws, screw it to the trapezoidal side piece.

Screw the two remaining side pieces together.

5 Put a small drop of glue into each screw hole, insert a plug, and gently pound the plugs into the holes with a mallet. Sand the plugs so that they're flush with the surface of the wood. If you're painting or staining the torchiere, do that now.

6 Test-fit the post cap.

Stand the torchiere up and test fit the post cap and the fuel canister.

7 Install the torchiere outdoors.

Pound one of the stakes about 12 in., or half of its length, into the ground with a mallet. Lay the torchiere, without the post cap and fuel canister, on the ground on one of its rectangular sides to gauge the distance between stakes. Pound the other stake into the ground.

Raise the upper end of the torchiere and slide it over the stakes.

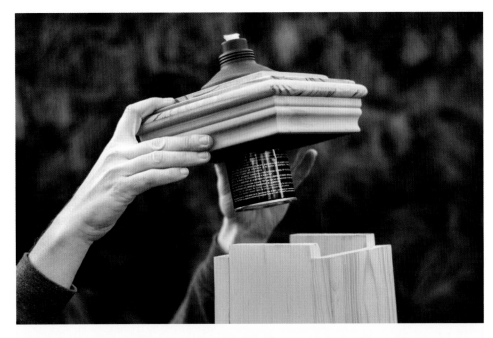

Rest the fuel canister in the post cap and place the post cap over the torchiere.

▲ The chair, ottoman, and lounger are perfect for a small gathering.

Sectional Furniture with Storage: Chair

28½ in. long × 21½ in. wide × 34 in. high

Between 1933 and 1942, America's Civilian Conservation Corps was responsible for, among other things, the design and construction of structures, buildings, and furniture for countless public works, many of which are in state and national parks. The term for the style of these structures in the National Park Service was "National Park Service Rustic," although the low buildings with horizontal lines, meant to be one with the landscape, evoked just as much 1930s modernism as it did rusticity.

It is with these gorgeous buildings and structures in mind that I created this sectional furniture. Simple pine structures, this chair, ottoman, and lounger nevertheless evoke a feeling of boxy modernism; the angled legs and seat back make the pieces look like they are going places (although with their sturdy structure they most certainly are not).

MATERIALS

Six 1 in. × 5 in. × 8 ft. boards

1¼-in. no. 8 deck screws

One 36-in. dowel with a ⁵⁄₁₆-in. diameter

Four 2-in. angle brackets

One 1 in. × 5 in. × 5 ft. length of scrap wood

One ½-in.-thick × 2 ft. × 4 ft. plywood project panel

Two 2-in. tee hinges

Weatherproof wood glue

Plugs

Paint or stain (optional)

One 20 in. × 20 in. × 3 in. seat cushion

One 20 in. × 20 in. × 2½ in. back cushion

TOOLS

Miter saw

Sander

Band saw or jigsaw

Adjustable square

Drill/driver

Quick-flip drive with a #8 ¹¹⁄₆₄-in. countersink bit

Framing square

Flat-sided clamps

Circular saw or jigsaw, for cutting plywood panels to size

Rubber mallet

▲ Pairing the chair with the ottoman makes two loungers.

The front legs of the chair are angled, ▶ and the space underneath the seat provides substantial storage.

Cut the side wall, front wall, back wall, and backrest pieces to length.

Set a stop on the miter saw at 27 in. Cut six 1 × 5 side wall pieces at 27 in. Set a stop on the miter saw at 21½ in. and cut eight 1 × 5 front wall, back wall, and backrest pieces at 21½ in. If it helps you stay organized, stack the boards according to size and label the stacks.

Sand the side wall pieces. **2**

Sand the edges but not the ends or corners of the side wall pieces. Sand the edges and ends of the front wall, back wall, and backrest pieces.

Cut the legs to length and shape. **3**

Cut two 1 × 5s to 17 in. for the front legs. Cut two 1 × 5s to 34 in. for the back legs.

Cut the legs to length and shape. (Continued)

Use a front leg to mark one back leg at 17 in.

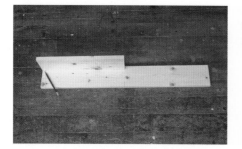

Stand a front leg piece on its edge and mark in from one corner at ¾ in.

Trace a line diagonally from one mark to the other.

Using a band saw or jigsaw, cut one back leg to shape.

Trace the shaped back leg onto the other, uncut back leg and cut it to shape.

Mark in from one corner along the front leg piece's width at ¾ in., and mark from the same corner along the piece's length at 4 in. Cut along the line. Trace that piece onto the other front leg, and cut that line as well.

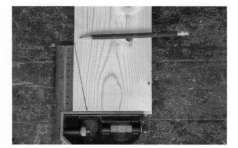

Arrange the legs and top side piece. **4**

Draw a line on one of the side wall pieces from end to end at ¾ in. in from the top edge.

4   **Arrange the legs and top side piece.** (Continued)

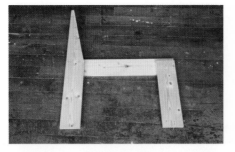

Place a back leg on top of the left end of the side wall piece. (You may need to put a piece of scrap wood underneath the back leg to keep it balanced.) Place a front leg on top of the right end of the side wall piece.

Align the top edge of the front leg with the line you've drawn on the side wall piece.

Align the line you've drawn halfway down the back leg piece with the line you've drawn on the side wall piece.

5   **Screw the legs to the side piece.**

Predrill for three counterbored holes in a triangular formation and screw three 1¼-in. screws into each leg, connecting the leg to the side wall piece. Use a framing square to check the legs for square.

Construct the other side. **6**

Repeat step 4 for the front and back legs and top side wall piece for the other side of the chair. Make sure the piece is facing the other direction!

Construct the other side of the chair following the directions in step 5. You should have two side assemblies for the chair facing opposite directions. Check for square.

Attach the remaining side pieces to each side. **7**

Put one of the side assemblies on a work surface with the screw holes facing up.

7 **Attach the remaining side pieces to each side.** (Continued)

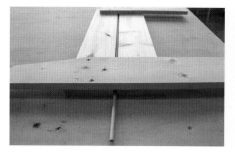

Put the dowel spacer below the top side wall piece (the one that's already attached to the legs), and position another side wall piece below it, aligning its ends with the outer edges of the legs. Predrill and screw two 1¼-in. screws into each leg piece where it contacts each side wall piece. Add a third side wall piece using the same method.

Repeat with the other side of the chair so that there are three side wall pieces on each side. The inside of the chair sides should look like this.

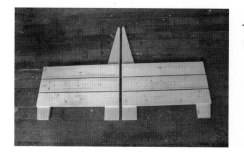

The outside of the chair sides should look like this.

Attach the angle brackets to the side assemblies. 8

Align two angle brackets with the inside bottom edge of the bottom side wall piece, about 1 in. from the inside of the leg. The screws that came with the brackets should be less than ¾ in. long. Screw them in place.

Cut and attach the seat supports. 9

Cut a piece of 5-in.-wide scrap wood down its length to make two pieces that are each 2½ in. wide. The length of both pieces should be shorter than the distance between the front and back legs. Align the top edge of the scrap piece with the line you drew ¾ in. from the top edge of the top side wall piece in step 4. Predrill and attach it to the inside of the top side wall piece with four 1¼-in. screws. Repeat with the other side assembly.

10   Add the front wall pieces.

Stand each side assembly on its back leg by clamping flat-sided clamps to the leg where it touches the floor.

On both ends of each of the three front pieces, mark ¾ in. in from each end and predrill for two counterbored holes between the lines you've marked and the ends of the pieces. Using 1⅝-in. screws, screw the front pieces to the ends of the side pieces.

The assembly should look like this.

Attach the backrest pieces.

On the two 21½-in.-long backrest pieces, mark ¾ in. in from the both ends, and then mark another ¾ in. in from that on the two backrest pieces. Predrill four holes in each piece between the lines you've marked.

Align the top edge of this piece with the top of the backrest and screw it in place using 1¼-in. screws.

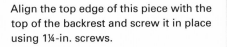

Use the dowel spacer to position the second backrest piece, then screw the backrest piece in place.

SECTIONAL FURNITURE WITH STORAGE: CHAIR

12 Add the back wall pieces.

Remove the clamps and stand the chair up with its front facing down (I stood the front of my chair on plywood to protect the front from being scratched by the floor). Mark ¾ in. in from both ends of the remaining three 21½-in. pieces. Predrill for two counterbored holes on each end of the face between the line you've marked and the ends of the piece. Using 1⅝-in. screws, screw the back wall pieces to the side walls, aligning them with the side pieces.

13 Cut the plywood to size for the seat and the floor of the storage space and attach the seat.

Using a jigsaw or a circular saw, cut two plywood rectangles to fit the inside of the chair. The rectangle for the floor of the storage space, which will rest on the angle brackets, should be 25 in. × 18½ in. The rectangle for the seat, which will rest on the seat supports, the top of the legs, and hinges, should be 19¾ in. × 22¼ in. There should be a small gap on all sides between the chair's frame and the floor of the storage area.

Place the floor of the storage space in the chair and rest it on the brackets.

Place the seat on the seat supports and the tops of the legs. The seat should fit between all the sides.

Attach the seat hinges. **14**

Center the seat between all sides, allowing enough room on the front edge for the hinges. Align the hinges so they sit flat on both surfaces (the round axle part should be on the inside) and position them about 2 in. from the sides of the chair. Screw the hinges in place.

Check to see that the seat lifts and sits down properly in its place.

Put a small drop of glue into each screw hole, insert a plug, and gently pound the plugs into the holes with a mallet. Sand the plugs so that they're flush with the surface of the wood. Paint or stain. **15**

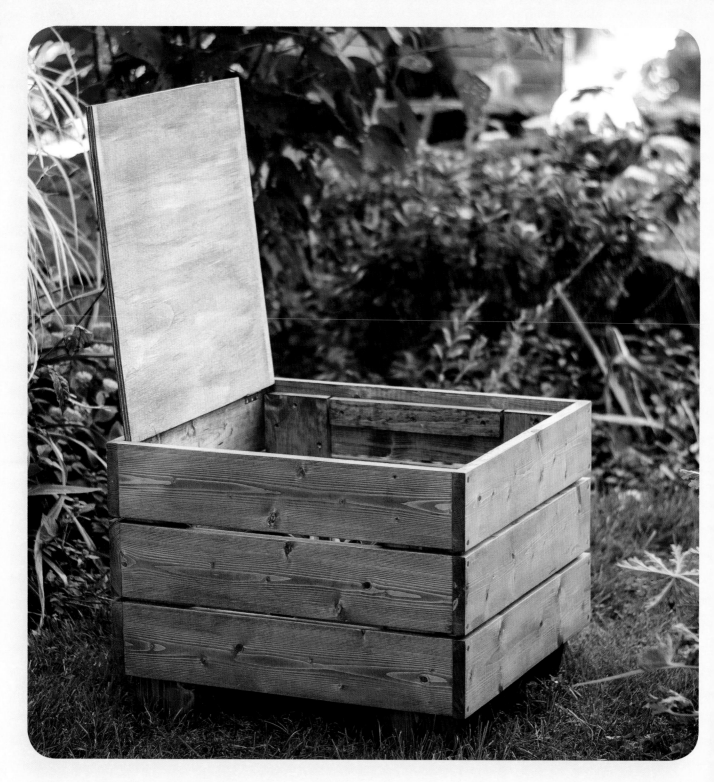

▲ Like the chair and lounger, the ottoman has storage
space under the seat.

Sectional Furniture with Storage: Ottoman

22¼ in. long × 21½ in. wide × 34 in. high

MATERIALS

Three 1 in. × 5 in. × 8 ft. boards

1¼-in. no. 8 deck screws

One 36-in. dowel with a ⁵⁄₁₆-in. diameter

Four 2-in. angle brackets

One 1 in. × 5 in. × 6 ft. length of scrap wood

One ½ in. × 2 ft. × 4 ft. foot plywood project panel

Two 2-in. tee hinges

Weatherproof wood glue

Plugs

Paint or stain (optional)

One 20 in. × 20 in. × 3 in. cushion

TOOLS

Miter saw

Adjustable square

Sander

Framing square

Drill/driver

Quick-flip drive with a #8 ¹¹⁄₆₄-in. countersink bit

Flat-sided clamps

Circular saw or jigsaw, for cutting plywood panels to size

Rubber mallet

1 Cut the front and back pieces to length.

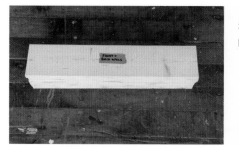

Set the miter saw at 21½ in. and cut six pieces of 1 × 5 at 21½ in.

2 Cut the side wall pieces to length.

Set the miter saw at 20¾ in. and cut six pieces of 1 × 5 at 20¾ in.

3 Cut the leg pieces to length and shape.

Cut four 1 × 5 boards at 17 in. Mark in from one corner along the board's width at ¾ in., and mark from the same corner along the board's length at 4 in. Draw a line from one mark to the other.

Using a miter saw, cut along the line you've drawn. Trace the shaped leg onto the other three leg pieces, and cut those pieces as well. Sand the face and edges of all the pieces.

Attach the legs to upper side wall pieces. **4**

Draw a line on one of the side wall pieces from end to end at ¾ in. from the top edge.

Position two leg pieces with their upper ends flush with the line you've drawn on the side wall piece, with the angled parts of the legs facing outward.

4 **Attach the legs to upper side wall pieces.** (Continued)

Predrill for three counterbored holes in a triangular formation for each leg. Use a square to make sure the leg is at 90 degrees from the side wall piece. Screw legs to side pieces with 1¼-in. screws. Attach the other leg to the side wall piece in the same manner.

Attach the remaining two legs to the other side wall piece in the same manner.

5 **Add the remaining side wall pieces.**

Place the dowel spacer against the lower edge of the upper side piece.

Place the second side wall piece next to the spacer, align the edges, and predrill two holes in each side and screw it into place. Repeat with the third side piece.

Repeat this process for the other side assembly. You'll have two sides that look like this.

Attach the angle brackets. 6

The angle brackets will hold the bottom of the box in place. Place the angle brackets on the insides of the legs, where they meet the lower edge of the side pieces, and screw them into place. The screws that came with the angle brackets should be less than ¾ in.

Cut and attach the seat supports. 7

Cut two pieces of scrap wood so that they fit between the two legs on each side assembly. They should be shorter than the distance between the legs. Place the seat supports so their top edge is flush with the line you drew in step 4, predrill three holes, and screw into place with 1¼-in. screws.

8 Attach the front and back pieces.

Mark ¾ in. in from both ends on the outside of the front and back pieces and predrill for two counterbored holes at each end.

Stand each side assembly up on its end, with a flat-sided clamp attached to one end to support it. The legs and hardware should be on the inside of the arrangement.

Position one front piece so that it spans the gap between the side assemblies. Predrill for counterbored holes and, using 1⅝-in. screws, screw one end into place on the side assembly.

Move the other side assembly so that it is aligned with the end of the front piece, and screw the pieces together.

Screw the second and third front pieces into place, aligning them with the side pieces.

Remove the clamps and turn the entire assembly over. Screw the three back pieces into place, aligning them with the side pieces.

Your assembly should look like this.

9 Cut the plywood to size for the seat and the floor of the storage space.

Using a jigsaw or a circular saw, cut one ½ in. × 19¾ in. × 19¾ in. and one ½ in. × 18 in. × 19¾ in. piece from plywood.

10 Position the floor of the storage space and attach the seat.

Stand the ottoman up on its feet. Place the ½ in. × 18 in. × 19¾ in. plywood floor on the angle brackets within.

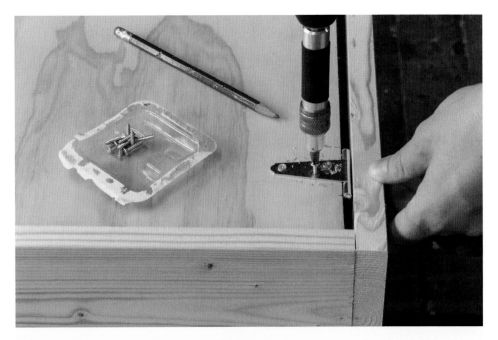

Place the plywood seat piece on top of the legs and seat supports. Position the hinges so both sides are flat against the wood and screw in place.

Put a small drop of glue into each screw hole, insert a plug, and gently pound the plugs into the holes with a mallet. Sand the plugs so that they're flush with the surface of the wood. Paint or stain.

11

▲ The finished lounger, perfect for relaxing on a summer day. Like the chair and ottoman, it has storage underneath.

Sectional Furniture with Storage: Lounger

49¼ in. long × 21½ in. wide × 34 in. high

MATERIALS

Five 1 in. × 5 in. × 8 ft. boards

Two 1 in. × 5 in. × 6 ft. boards

1¼-in. no.8 deck screws

One 36-in. dowel with a ⁵⁄₁₆-in. diameter

Six 2-in. angle brackets

Four scrap pieces for seat supports

Two ½ in. × 2 ft. × 4 ft. plywood project panels

Two 2-in. tee hinges

Weatherproof wood glue

Plugs

Paint or stain (optional)

Two 20 in. × 20 in. × 3 in. seat cushions

One 20 in. × 20 in. × 2½ in. back cushion

TOOLS

Miter saw

Sander

Framing square

Drill/driver

Quick-flip drive with a #8 ¹¹⁄₆₄-in. countersink bit

Flat-sided clamps

Circular saw or jigsaw

Rubber mallet

1   Cut the front wall, back wall, backrest, and leg pieces to length.

From the 8-ft. boards, cut eight 1 × 5s at 21½ in. These are the front wall, back wall, and backrest pieces. Cut six 1 × 5s at 47¾ in. These are the side wall pieces. From the 6-ft. boards, cut four 1 × 5s at 17 in. These are the front and middle legs. Cut two 1 × 5s at 34 in. These are the back legs. Sand all the pieces.

2   Shape the front, middle, and back legs.

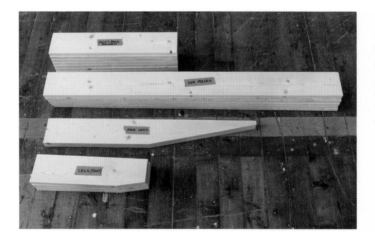

See step 3 in the Sectional Chair project for instructions on how to shape the legs. The middle legs for the lounger should be the same shape as the front legs for the Sectional Chair.

Arrange and attach the legs to the upper side piece.

Mark a line along the length of one of the side wall pieces at ¾ in. from the top edge. Center the top end of a middle leg on this line, with the angled corner at the bottom, facing to the right. Position a front leg at the right-hand end of the side wall piece, with the top end of the front leg also at the ¾-in. line and the angled corner also at the bottom, facing right. Position a back leg at the left edge of the side wall piece, with the line you drew on it aligned with the ¾-in. line on the side wall piece, and the angled part facing right. Use a square to make sure the legs are 90 degrees from the side wall piece. The lower end of the three leg pieces should all be the same distance from the side wall piece.

Predrill for three counterbored holes for each leg, in a triangular formation, and screw the legs, using 1¼-in. screws, to the side piece.

3 Arrange and attach the legs to the upper side piece. (Continued)

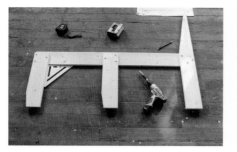

Repeat step 3 with the other side wall piece, with the pieces facing the other direction.

4 Attach the remaining side pieces.

Place the side assembly on the work surface with the side piece facing down. Use the dowel spacer to place the next side piece, and attach the legs to this side piece. Add the third side wall piece, again using the spacer. Repeat the process with the other side assembly, until all six side pieces have been attached.

5 Attach the angle brackets.

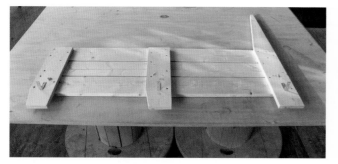

Screw one angle bracket to the inside of each leg, centered between the side edges of the legs and at the same level as the bottom of the lower side piece.

Attach the side supports. **6**

Between every leg, ¾ in. from the top of the upper side piece, attach a piece of scrap wood to support the seat. You'll have two side supports on the left and right side assemblies of the lounger.

Predrill and attach the front, backrest, and back pieces. **7**

On both ends of the face of each of the three front and back pieces, measure and mark ¾ in. in from each end and predrill for two counterbored holes.

Stand both side assemblies on their back ends on the floor and use flat-sided clamps to stabilize the assemblies. Align the top front piece with the ends of the side wall pieces and screw into place using 1⅝-in. screws. Attach the second and third front pieces in the same manner.

7 Predrill and attach the front, backrest, and back pieces. (Continued)

On the two backrest pieces, mark ¾ in. in from both ends, and then measure and mark ¾ in. in from the line you just drew. Predrill two holes in both ends of the faces of each piece inside the lines you drew. Align a backrest piece with the upper ends of the back legs. Screw in place using 1¼-in. screws.

Use the dowel to place the second backrest piece. Screw in place.

Screw the three back pieces in place.

Cut the floor and seat pieces to size and attach the seat with hinges.

8

From plywood panels, cut the floor piece to 42¾ in. × 18 in. Cut the seat piece to 42¾ in. × 19¾ in. Place the plywood floor on the angle brackets. Attach the seat piece with hinges, using the same technique shown in step 14 of the sectional chair project (see page 175).

Put a small drop of glue into each screw hole, insert a plug, and gently pound the plugs into the holes with a mallet. Sand the plugs so that they're flush with the surface of the wood. Paint or stain.

9

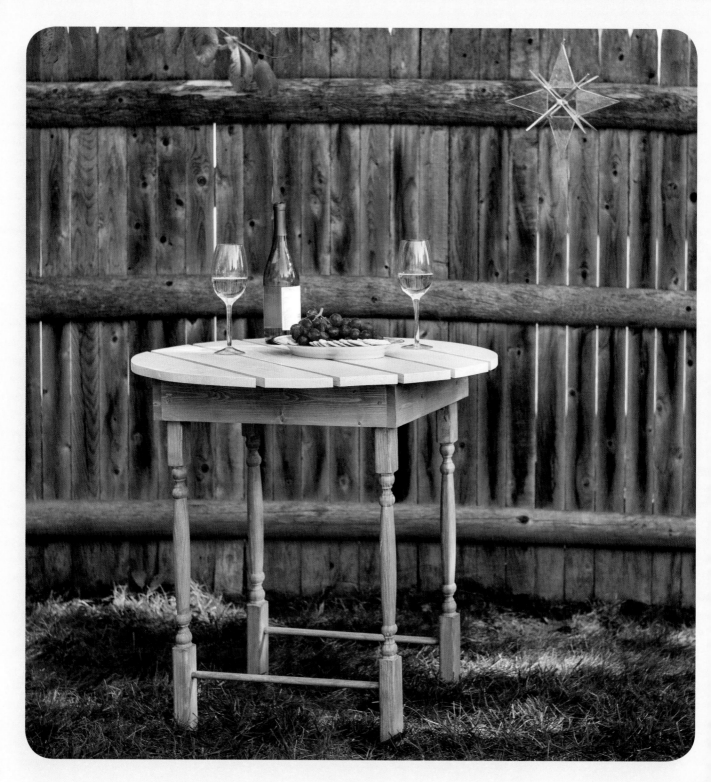

▲ The finished bistro table. The legs are cut from staircase spindles and strengthened by horizontal dowels on two sides.

Bistro Table

29 in. diameter × 29 in. wide × 30 in. high

This small, cottage-style table is perfect for enjoying an evening outdoors with some wine and cheese. Pair this table with two stools or folding bistro-style chairs—the table suits two people perfectly. The tabletop pieces are spaced so that rain and snow don't accumulate on top, and they are angled over the apron so that each piece gets the maximum amount of support from the apron.

I used outdoor, pressure-treated staircase spindles for the legs. Use any design of 3-inch spindle or board you like as long as the tops and bottoms are rectangular (so you can drill holes for the leg supports and attach the tops to the apron). Pressure-treated spindles are more rot-resistant, but are also more toxic to work with—be sure to wear a dust mask when cutting, drilling, or making sawdust with pressure-treated wood.

MATERIALS

One 1 in. × 4 in. × 8 ft. board

1⅝-in. no. 8 deck screws

Two 1 in. × 5 in. × 8 ft. boards

Weatherproof wood glue

Plugs

Four 2 in. × 3 in. × 36 in. spindles

One 48-in. dowel with a ⅝-in. diameter

Paint (optional)

TOOLS

Miter saw

Drill/driver

Quick-flip drive with a #8 11⁄64-in. countersink bit

½-in. drill bit

Clamps

One 36-in. dowel with a ½-in. diameter

Framing square

Band saw

Scrap wood, at least 16-in. long (for the compass)

Jigsaw or coping saw

Rubber mallet

Sander

Sandpaper

Adjustable square

Drill press

Masking tape

⅝-in. drill bit

1   Construct the apron.

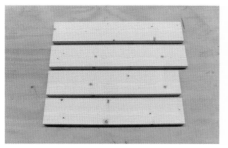

From the 1 × 4, cut two 20-in. lengths and two 18½-in. lengths.

2   Mark the two 20-in. boards for screw holes.

Trace the edge of another board on both ends of the faces of the two 20-in. boards.

Mark two screw holes in the area you traced at both ends of the two longer boards and predrill for counterbored holes.

Attach a clamp to the work surface and set one of the 18½-in. pieces on its edge, abutting the clamp. Using 1⅝-in. screws, attach one of the 20-in. boards to the 18½-in. board.

Repeat with the other two boards, forming a square. This is the apron for the table.

Cut the tabletop pieces to length. **3**

From the 1 × 5s cut two 31-in. pieces, two 30-in. pieces, and two 23-in. pieces.

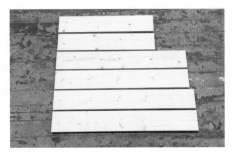

Painting the Table

If you decide to paint the table, paint the sides of the tabletop pieces after you've cut them to size but before you attach them to the apron. It's easier to paint them at this point, before they've been screwed to the apron, rather than try to push a paintbrush in between the pieces after they've been attached to the apron.

4   **Attach the two longest tabletop pieces to the apron.**

Place the two 31-in. tabletop pieces on the work surface, with the ½-in. dowel spacer between them.

Center two opposite corners of the apron over the spacer. The corners of the apron should be the same distance from the ends of the tabletop pieces, about 1⅜ in.

Trace the inside and outside of the apron on the two tabletop pieces.

The tracing should look like this.

Mark and predrill two holes inside each of the traced lines on each board. You'll have four holes per board.

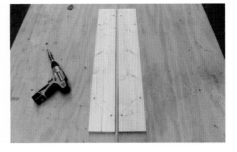

Place the two tabletop pieces on top of the apron, with the traced lines facing up, and with the spacer between them. and attach using 1⅝-in. screws.

5 **Attach the next two tabletop pieces.**

Turn the tabletop assembly over so its tabletop pieces are on the work surface. Place the dowel spacer underneath the apron next to one of the attached tabletop pieces. Place one of the 30-in. tabletop pieces next to the dowel, with the tabletop piece's ends centered under the apron. The 30-in. piece should be ½-in. from the ends of the 31-in. pieces.

Trace the outline of the apron on this piece. Place the other 30-in. piece on the other side, again using the dowel spacer, and center the piece under the apron and trace.

Mark for holes and predrill. Turn the tabletop assembly over.

Screw the tabletop pieces in place, using the dowel spacer to keep the pieces the correct distance from each other.

Attach the two 23-in. tabletop pieces.

Repeat the process with the two 23-in. pieces, still using the dowel spacer. The ends of the 23-in. pieces should be 3½ in. from the ends of the 30-in. pieces.

The tabletop should look like this.

Create a compass and use it to draw a circle on the tabletop. **7**

Using a band saw or coping saw, cut a small notch in the end of a 16-in. piece of scrap wood, large enough to fit the tip of a pencil.

Create a compass and use it to draw a circle on the tabletop. (Continued)

Place the notched scrap wood on the tabletop so that the notch is flush with the edge of one of the outermost boards.

Measure and mark the center of the tabletop on the scrap wood. (The center of the tabletop will be in the space between the two middle tabletop pieces.)

Drill a ½-in. hole in the center mark on the scrap board. Place the ½-in. dowel spacer in the hole and in between the boards in the center of the tabletop. Use the notch in the spacer to hold the pencil and draw a 30-in.-diameter circle around the tabletop. The circle should hit both edges of the outermost pieces and be outside the corners of the apron.

Cut the tabletop into a circle. 8

Clamp the tabletop to a corner of the work surface. (You'll have to move the clamps as you cut around the outside). Using a jigsaw or coping saw, cut around the circle.

You should have a round tabletop.

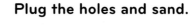

Plug the holes and sand. 9

Put a small drop of glue into each screw hole, insert a plug, and gently pound the plugs into the holes with a mallet. Sand the plugs so that they're flush with the surface of the wood. Sand the tabletop.

Sand the edges of the tabletop and the corners in between the tabletop pieces as well, using a folded quarter-sheet of sandpaper.

10 Construct the legs.

The legs have a 2-in. edge and a 3-in. face. Cut the legs to 29 in. You may cut a piece off both ends or just one end—it's an aesthetic decision—as long as you leave at least 4 in. of a rectangular end at the top of all four legs for them to be attached to the apron and some space near the bottom for the dowels.

On the 3-in.-wide face of each leg, mark a centered hole 5 in. up from the bottom.

If you're using a drill press, set the depth of the cut at ½ in. from the table. If you're using a handheld drill, mark the ⅝-in. drill bit with tape at ⅞ in. from the bottom of the drill bit. Stop drilling when the mark is even with the board.

Drill one ⅝-in.-wide, ⅞-in.-deep hole in each leg. The hole will not go all the way through the leg.

Cut the ⅝-in. dowel into two 17½ in. pieces. Put the dowels in the holes in the spindles. The distance from the outside of each leg should be 18½ in., the same length as the inside of the apron—if the distance isn't correct, the legs won't be vertical and parallel to each other. Once you know the assembly is the correct size, remove the dowels, place a dab of glue in each hole, and reinsert the dowels into the holes. You may need to pound the dowels in with a mallet.

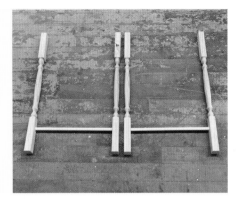

Attach the legs to the table. 11

Place the tabletop facedown on the work surface and nestle the legs into the corners. Mark and predrill holes on the outside of the apron on the two sides of each leg that sit in the corner. There should be two screw holes vertically centered where the apron meets the 3-in. face of each leg (next to where the existing screws are), and one screw hole in the center where the apron meets the 2-in. edge of each leg.

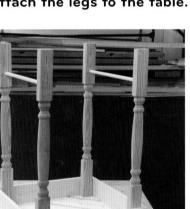

One at a time, clamp and screw the legs to the apron. After you've screwed one screw into each leg to the tabletop, use a framing square to check that the legs are 90 degrees from the tabletop, then screw the other two screws into each leg.

12 Put a small drop of glue into each screw hole, insert a plug, and gently pound the plugs into the holes with a mallet. Sand the plugs so that they're flush with the surface of the wood.

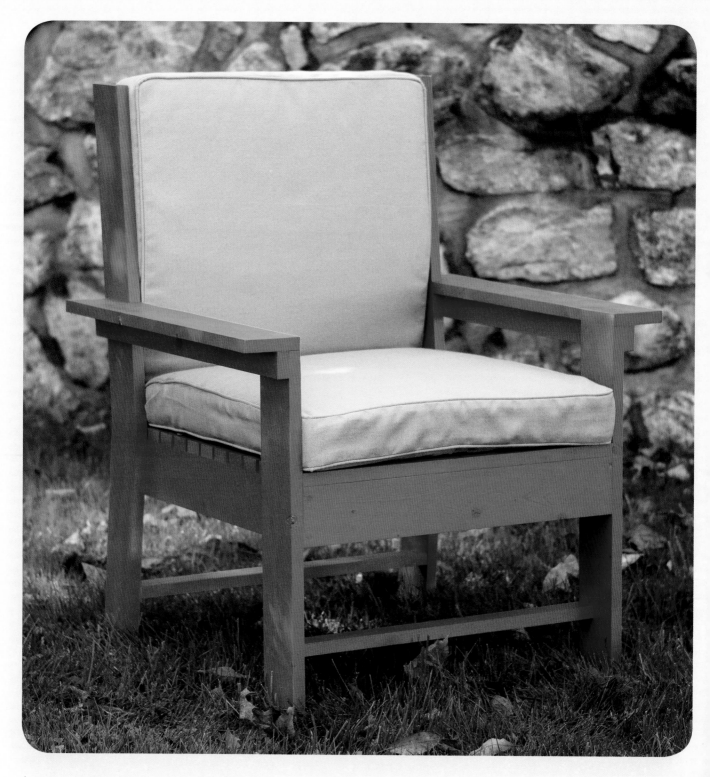

▲ The International Orange chair with a light blue cushion adds a pop of color to this garden.

International Orange Chair

28 in. wide × 21 in. high × 26 in. deep

This is one of my favorite projects in this book: the chair is sturdy and jaunty at the same time. The chevron-shaped angle in the back suggests forward movement when viewed from the side, while the horizontal bars give it a stationary feel when viewed from the front or back.

I chose to use a color that pops, hence the chair's name: I painted the chair International Orange, the same color as the Golden Gate Bridge, and used an azure cushion, the color of the sky behind the bridge on a sunny day in San Francisco. For a more restful color choice, use a deep brown stain and a taupe-striped cushion; for a beachy look, paint it white and use a colorful patterned cushion. I used spray paint after construction, but prepainting is also an option.

MATERIALS

Two 1 in. × 4 in. × 8 ft. boards

1⅝-in. no. 8 deck screws

Scrap wood

Weatherproof wood glue

Four 1 in. × 2 in. × 6 ft. boards

1¼-in. no. 8 deck screws

Plugs

One 1 in. × 6 in. × 6 ft. board

Masking tape

Paint or stain (optional)

One 21 in. × 20 in. × 23-in.-high × 4-in.-thick cushion

TOOLS

Miter saw

Drill/driver

Quick-flip drive with a #8 ¹¹⁄₆₄-in. countersink bit

Sander

One 24-in. dowel spacer with a diameter of ⅜ in.

Speed square

Rubber mallet

Jigsaw or band saw

Coping saw

To give it a softer appearance, like that of a classic Adirondack chair, curve the back legs rather than angle them, round the front of the armrests, and don't use a cushion. The chair is quite comfortable without one. The chair can also be made without armrests: cut the front legs at 15 inches and add a stretcher from the center of the front stretcher to the center of the back stretcher. I liked the look of many thin slats on the seat and back, but using fewer, wider slats for the seat and back saves time and screws.

 Construct the seat apron.

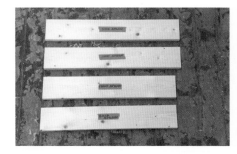

Using the miter saw, cut two pieces from one of the 1 × 4s at 22 in. These pieces are the two side aprons. Cut two pieces of a 1 × 4 at 21 in. These pieces are the front and back aprons.

Trace the end of a side piece onto the front and back aprons and mark for two holes. Predrill for counterbored holes on the front and back aprons and use 1⅝-in. screws to attach the front and back aprons to the side aprons.

Cut two triangular pieces of scrap wood (make sure they have a perfect 90-degree angle) and attach them to the inside front of the frame using glue and 1⅝-in. screws.

The triangles will prevent the rectangle of the apron from racking, or going out of square.

Cut the seat slats and back slats. 2

Cut nineteen slats out of 1 × 2s at 21 in.—the same length as the front and back aprons. Sand the edges and faces. Set six slats aside for the back slats. The remaining thirteen will be the seat slats.

Attach the seat slats to the apron. 3

To help prevent racking, I used four holes (two at each end) on the two outside slats and the middle slat, and I used two holes (one at each end) for the rest of the slats. Predrill two holes at both ends of three seat slats (the seat back slats will be attached differently; do not predrill them). Use these slats for the first, middle, and last slats. Predrill two holes, one at each end, in the remaining seat slats. Align the first slat with the front face of the apron and attach using four 1¼-in. screws. Place the dowel spacer on the apron next to the first seat slat and place a second seat slat snugly against it and screw in place.

3   Attach the seat slats to the apron. (Continued)

Attach the rest of the seat slats, periodically using a speed square to check the apron for square and adjusting as necessary. Place a drop of glue in each hole, plug, and sand flush. It is easier to plug and sand the seat now rather than later, when it's attached to the arms.

Smooth Seats and Arms

To sand outdoor furniture, I usually end with 100- or 120-grit sandpaper for seat and bench surfaces and armrests.

4   Cut the front and back legs to length.

Cut two 1 × 4s at 22 in. for the front legs. Cut two 1 × 6s at 36 in. for the back legs. Use a marker and masking tape to label the pieces. Arrange all four legs vertically on the work surface. Mark a horizontal line on all four legs at 15 in. up from the bottom. This marks the top of the seat.

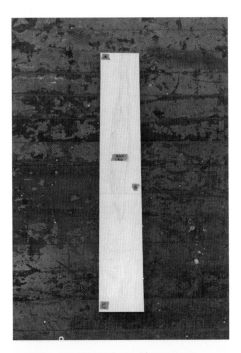

Use a marker and masking tape to label the upper left corner of one of the back legs A. Label the right end of the 15-in. line B. Label the lower left corner C.

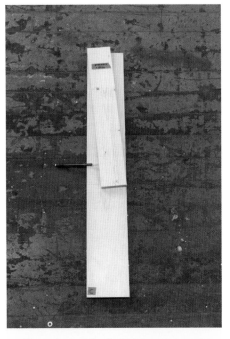

Place one of the front legs on top of the back leg so that its top left corner aligns with point A and its bottom right corner aligns with point B. Trace the front leg's sides and bottom onto the back leg.

Place the front leg so that its top right corner aligns with point B and its left side intersects point C and trace its sides onto the back leg.

5 **Cut the back legs to shape.** (Continued)

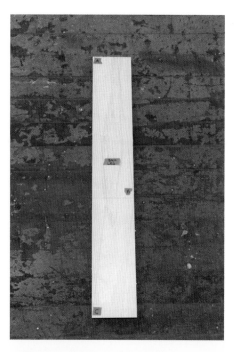

You should have a right-facing boomerang shape.

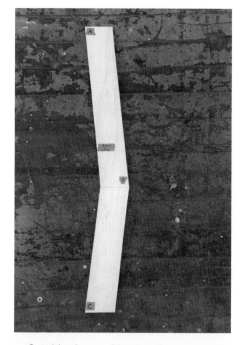

Cut this shape with a band saw or jigsaw.

Sand the edges.

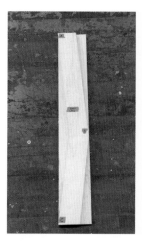

Trace the first back leg onto the second, cut, and sand.

Place one back leg and one front leg on the work surface. To ensure the two left corners of the back leg stay vertical, place the back leg so that point A is on the left edge of the work surface and point C is on the lower left corner. Align the bottom of the front leg with the edge of the work surface.

Place the seat sideways on the legs, with the top edge of the slats at the 15-in. marks.

Use a square to ensure the front leg is 90 degrees from the apron. Predrill, from the inside of the side apron, three holes to go into each leg. Attach the side apron to the legs using 1¼-in. screws.

6   Attach the legs to the seat. (Continued)

Flip the assembly over and attach the other side apron to the other two legs.

The chair assembly should look like this.

Cut and attach the front and back leg stretchers. ⑦

Measure the distance between the insides of the legs. Cut two 1 × 2 leg stretchers to that length. (For this project, the distance should be 24 in., but you might have a slightly different result.)

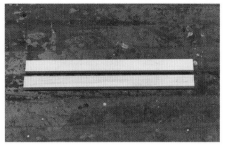

Mark the inside and outside of all four legs at 4 in. and 4¾ in. from the bottom. The stretchers will sit in between the lines you've drawn. The back side of the front stretcher will sit flush with the back side of the front legs, and the front side of the back stretcher will sit flush with the front side of the back legs.

From the outside of each leg, mark and predrill for two counterbored holes inside the lines you've drawn. Attach the leg stretchers using 1⅝-in. screws.

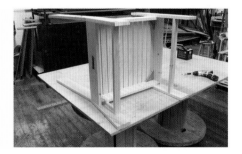

7 Cut and attach the front and back leg stretchers. (Continued)

With the stretchers in place, the assembly should look like this.

8 Make and attach the armrest supports.

Place the chair on its side on the work surface. Slide a piece of scrap wood under the lower part of the legs. Slide the 1 × 2 you'll be using as an armrest support underneath the upper part of the legs. Align the upper front corner of the 1 × 2 with the upper front corner of the front leg. Using a square, check that the length of the 1 × 2 arm support is 90 degrees from the length of the front leg. Trace the outer side of the back leg onto the 1 × 2. The line will be slightly angled, about 7 degrees. The 1 × 2 armrest support should be about 24 in. at its longest.

Using a miter saw set at the same angle as the line, cut the 1 × 2 on the line you traced.

Set the miter saw back at its usual 0 degree setting. Make an identical armrest support by tracing the first armrest support onto the off-cut piece (the angle of the off-cut piece will also be correct) and cut the other end of this piece at a right angle.

From the inside of the legs, predrill for three counterbored holes in a triangular formation in each leg and attach the armrest support pieces with 1¼-in. screws.

With the armrest supports in place, the assembly should look like this.

9 Attach the armrests.

I used wide armrests for the comfort of the sitter and to provide a surface for a drink or paperback. If you do not want to use wide armrests, sand the edges and corners of the armrest supports well and move ahead to step 10.

Cut two 1 × 4s at 24 in. for the armrests. Cut a notch in the armrests for the seat back to fit in: place one armrest on top of an armrest support, aligning the front edge of the armrest with the front edge of the armrest support, and trace the 7-degree angle of the back leg on the side of the armrest.

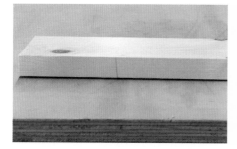

The line you've drawn, with the 7-degree angle traced from the back leg, should look like this.

Using a square, continue the line on the face of the armrest ¾ in. in from the edge.

Trace a piece of nominally 1-in.-thick scrap wood with the same thickness as the leg from the line you've drawn to the back end of the armrest.

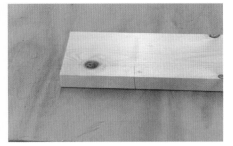

Use a coping saw to cut the shorter, 7-degree angled line from the edge of the piece of wood. Then use a band saw to cut the longer line from the end of the piece of wood.

Place the notched armrest on the armrest support to ensure it fits.

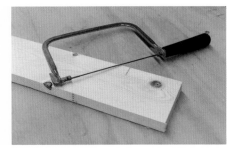

Predrill for six counterbored holes and attach the armrest with 1⅝-in. screws. The second screw from the front should go into the front leg; the other five screws should go into the armrest support. Repeat with the other armrest.

10 Attach the backrest slats.

Retrieve the six backrest slats. Fit one backrest slat on the upper back side of the back legs, flush with the top ends. Predrill the outside of the back legs for two screws on each end of the slat. Attach the uppermost backrest piece using 1¼-in. screws.

Place the dowel spacer between the uppermost backrest slat and the next one. Predrill and screw. Continue spacing, predrilling, and screwing all the pieces.

11 Put a small drop of glue into each screw hole, insert a plug, and gently pound the plugs into the holes with a mallet. Sand the plugs so that they're flush with the surface of the wood. Paint or stain (or touch up if you decided to do so before construction).

The finished chaise longue, poolside. The backrest
adjusts to four different positions.

Chaise Longue

25½ in. wide × 12¼ in. high × 78 in. long

A simple, rectangular chaise longue with tapered corner brace legs has a modern feel; to personalize the style of yours, cut the legs to any shape you like as long as you leave at least 2 inches on the bottom end of each side. For a classic look, cut curves, or for a boxy look, don't cut them at all. I gave mine an angle for a midcentury-modern look.

Although the plain wood is quite relaxing for lounging upon, I built mine for a cushion. Chaise longue cushions come in all different sizes. Adjust the dimensions to your own cushion: cut the seat slats to the cushion's width and cut the length of the outer sides to the cushion's length plus 1½ inches. The width of the last seat slat may need to be adjusted to fit your customized length.

MATERIALS

Eight 1 in. × 4 in. × 8 ft. boards

One 1 in. × 6 in. × 2 ft. board

Two 1 in. × 3 in. × 8 ft. boards

1¼-in. no. 8 deck screws

1⅝-in. no. 8 deck screws

Four 2-in. T-strap hinges

½-in. or ¾-in. screws for the hinges

One 48-in. dowel with a ¾-in. diameter

1⅝-in. no. 8 deck screws

Weatherproof wood glue

Plugs

Paint or stain (optional)

One 24 in. × 48 in. × 4 in. seat cushion

One 24 in. × 30 in. × 4 in. back cushion

TOOLS

Miter saw

Drill/driver

Quick-flip drive with a #8 ^{11}/₆₄-in. countersink bit

¾-in. drill bit

Band saw, scroll saw, or coping saw

Sander with 60-grit and 100-grit sandpaper

One 24-in. (or longer) dowel with a ⅜-in. diameter

Tape measure

Drill press (optional)

1⅛-in. drill bit

Rubber mallet

1   Cut the outer frame pieces, end frame pieces, and leg pieces to length.

From the 1 × 4s, cut two outer frame pieces to 78 in. and two end frame pieces to 24 in. From the 1 × 6, cut eight leg pieces to 11¾ in.

2   Mark the outer frame.

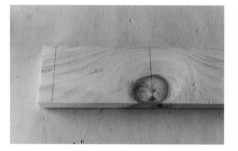

Arrange the outer frame and end frame pieces in a rectangle, with the ends of the end frame pieces abutting the outer sides of the outer frame pieces. Trace the end frame pieces onto the outer frame pieces. The line will be ¾ in. from either end of both outer frame pieces.

Position one leg piece on one outer frame piece, with its edge on the line you have just drawn. Trace the width of the leg piece onto the outer frame piece.

Mark the width of one nominally 1-in.-wide board all the way along the upper edge of each outer frame piece. This line indicates where the seat slats will go.

Measure and mark 30 in. from one end of each outer frame piece. The 30-in. mark indicates where the backrest will begin. (Adjust if you are using a cushion with different dimensions.) The remaining 48-in. are the seat.

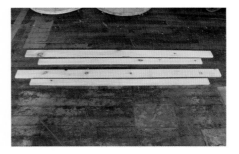

Cut the inner frame pieces to length and attach to the outer frame. 3

From the 1 × 3, cut the inner frame pieces. The length of the inner frame should be the length of the space between the two leg markings on the two outer frame pieces; for this chaise the length was 65⁹⁄₁₆ in.

Align the inner frame inside the marks for the seat slats and the legs. Predrill for counterbored holes and attach it to the outer frame, using 1¼-in. screws about every 4 in.

4 Construct the frame.

Mark and predrill for counterbored holes from the outside of the outer frame assemblies. Using 1⅝-in. screws, attach the two outer frame assemblies to the two end frame pieces, making sure the two outer frame assemblies are a mirror image of each other.

5 Cut the leg pieces to shape.

On one of the leg pieces, make a mark along the right edge 2½ in. from the upper right corner. Make another mark along the bottom end 3½ in. from the lower left corner. Trace a straight edge between these two marks and, using the band saw, cut. Trace this piece onto the seven other leg pieces and cut.

6 Construct the leg brackets.

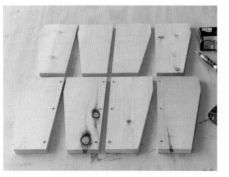

Each leg consists of a bracket made of two leg pieces. Arrange the eight leg pieces in two rows, with the two left pieces in each row facing the left and the two right pieces in each row facing the right. Draw a line ¾ in. in from the straight side of the four pieces in the bottom row. On each piece in the bottom row, predrill for three counterbored holes between the line and the edge of the piece.

Using 1¼-in. screws, attach the straight edge of each piece in the bottom row to the straight edge of its mate in the top row. You should have four leg brackets.

Cut and sand the seat slats. 7

From the 1 × 4s, cut twelve seat slats at 24 in. Sand one face and the corners of the edges of each seat slat. (Don't sand the corners at the ends because they'll abut the outer frame.)

Attach the seat slats to the inner frame. 8

Predrill for four counterbored holes on the sanded side of each slat, two holes at each end.

Attach the seat slats to the inner frame. (Continued)

Place the ⅜-in. dowel spacer on the line you drew between the seat and the backrest. Place the first seat slat, sanded side up, next to the spacer on the side of the dowel where the seat begins. Screw the seat slat to the inner frame.

Move the ⅜-in. dowel spacer to the other side of the first seat slat and put the second seat slat in place. Predrill for four counterbored holes and screw the second seat slat to the inner frame. At this point, check the frame to make sure the corners are 90 degrees by using a tape measure to measure the distance from the frame's opposing corners. If the measurements are the same, then the frame assembly is 90 degrees. If they're not the same, slightly push in the two opposite corners that are the longer distance from each other and check again to see if the distance between the opposite corners is the same.

Keep using the dowel spacer to attach the seat slats. Leave the last seat slat off until step 13, in order to have something to grab when you need to move the assembly.

Cut and sand the backrest pieces. 9

From a 1 × 3, cut and label two backrest support pieces at 26½ in.

From a 1 × 3, cut and label two backrest stand pieces at 18 in.

From a 1 × 4, cut and label two backrest stop pieces at 27 in.

From a 1 × 4, cut six backrest slats at 23¾ in.

Cut the 1 × 6 at 23¾ in.

Sand one face and all the corners of the backrest slats.

Cut a handle in the largest backrest slat. 10

In the 1 × 6 backrest slat, drill two 1⅛-in. holes, centered at 10½ in. from either end of the backrest slat. The holes should almost abut one edge of the slat. Mark lines from the edge of each circle to the outside of the board, and from the edge of one circle to the other.

Cut along the line with a band saw, scroll saw, or coping saw to form a handle. Sand the handle until it feels smooth to the touch.

Construct the backrest.

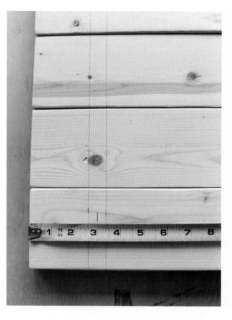

On the sanded face of each of the 1 × 4 backrest slats, mark four lines: at 2⅝ in. from either end and at 3⅜ in. from either end. These lines indicate where the backrest supports will be. Mark for two screw holes between each pair of lines, for a total of four screw holes per backrest slat. The screw holes will be 3 in. from either end. Predrill for counterbored holes.

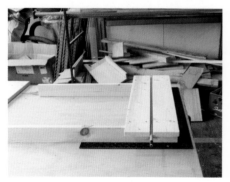

Position the two 27-in. backrest supports on the work surface. Using 1⅝-in. screws, attach the face of one backrest slat (sanded side up) to the edge of the supports. The edge of the first slat should be aligned with the end of the supports, and the rest of the slats should be spaced using the ⅜-in. dowel. Predrill and attach the slat with the cutout handle last, at the end of the backrest support with the handle facing the outside.

Hinge the backrest to the seat slats. **12**

Place the backrest in the frame. Use the ⅜-in. dowel to properly space the backrest slats from the seat slats. Place two hinges about 1 in. from each end to connect the backrest slats to the seat slats. Attach the hinges using ½-in. screws.

With the backrest in place, the chaise longue should look like this.

Attach the legs. **13**

Clean the dust off the work surface and turn the chaise lounge over.

Place the legs upside down in their spaces at the four corners of the upside down frame. The legs on the end with the missing seat slat will need to be propped in place with a nominally 1-in.-thick (actually ¾ in.) piece of scrap wood.

Predrill for six counterbored holes in each leg bracket, three on each piece of the bracket. Use 1¼-in. screws to attach the leg brackets to the inside of the outer frame. Place the chaise longue, right side up, on the floor and attach the last seat slat.

14 Construct the backrest stand.

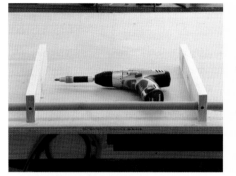

Cut the ¾-in. dowel to 22 in. Measure and mark at 3 in. and 3¾ in. in from each end of the 48-in. dowel. Drill a ¾-in. hole in each backrest stand piece, the center of which should be 9/16 in. from one end. Insert the dowel into the holes and align with the marks. Predrill and screw a 1⅝-in. screw into the end of each backrest stand piece so that the screw holds the dowel in place.

15 Hinge the backrest stand to the backrest.

Fold the backrest over so that the backside is facing up. Place the stand on the back of the backrest, so that the dowel sits above the ends of the backrest supports. Mark ⅝ in. from the edge of the outermost backrest slat and place the ends of the stand pieces on this line.

Hinge the other end of the two backrest stand pieces to the back of the third backrest slat. Test the hinge mechanism. (One end of my dowel was too close to the end of the backrest support, so I cut off the corner of the backrest support with a coping saw to make it fit.)

The assembly should now have legs, seat slats, backrest slats, and the backrest stand.

Cut the backrest stops to shape. 16

Measure and mark for four holes in both backrest stop pieces, centered at ¾ in., 2½ in., 4 in., and 7 in. from the end.

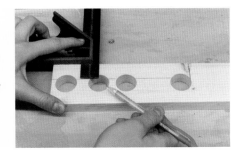

Drill each hole with a 1⅛-in.-diameter bit. Draw a line through the holes 1 in. from the top edge of one backrest stop piece. The line will intersect the circles a little above the center. Draw another line from the outside of the innermost circle, vertically to the edge of the board.

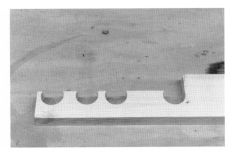

Using a band saw or coping saw, cut these lines.

16   Cut the backrest stops to shape. (Continued)

Using a band saw or coping saw, round over the innermost edges, so they look like waves crashing in from the end of the board. The rounded edges will smooth the movement of adjusting the backrest.

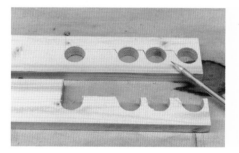

Trace this shape onto the other backrest stop and cut using a band saw.

17   Attach the backrest stops.

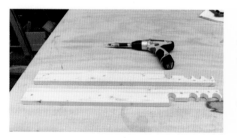

Place the backrest stop pieces on the work surface, with the holes facing opposite directions. Predrill for seven holes in each stop: one screw at the bottom of each wave, and three screws along the rest of the board.

Using 1⅝-in. screws and, optionally, glue, attach the backrest stops to the inner frame piece, with the wave end of the board abutting the inside of the leg.

Glue

I chose to use glue and screws when attaching the backrest stops because I imagined the wave parts breaking along the grain after being exposed to a few years of precipitation. Using glue is optional. If you choose to use glue, attach the backrest stops with two screws and test the mechanism first before applying glue.

Test the backrest mechanism. **18**

The backrest should lie flat in the down position. This is the first backrest stop.

The second, third, and fourth backrest stops allow the backrest to be positioned at different angles.

Put a small drop of glue into each screw hole, insert a plug, and gently pound them into the holes with a mallet. Sand the plugs so that they're flush with the surface of the wood. Paint or stain. **19**

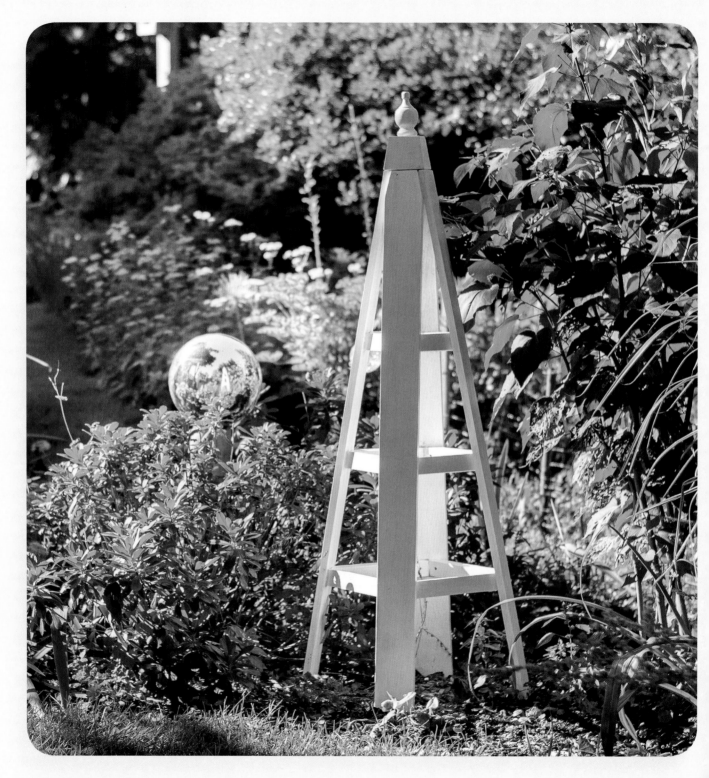

▲ The finished obelisk.

Obelisk

20½ in. diagonally across its base, 55 in.
high, including ornament

Train climbing plants up the sides of this obelisk or
leave it bare as an objet d'art wherever your garden
needs height. Depending on what type of plant you'd
like to climb your trellis, you may want to fasten small
eyehooks every 4 inches up the outside.

Choose any decorative shape you like to adorn the top.
The obelisk I originally made used only one bun foot
with a craft finial; after I finished building it I decided
to extend the lines of the obelisk by adding a second
bun foot on top of the first, and I put the craft finial on
top of the second bun foot. For a more modern look,
leave the top of the obelisk undecorated.

The rails (the horizontal pieces) in this project are cut
at compound miters, at 5 degrees in one direction and
45 degrees in the other direction. Using arrows to
mark the pieces and checking the cuts against the
obelisk's stiles (the vertical pieces) makes it easy to
ensure the rails are trapezoids, not parallelograms.

MATERIALS

Two 1 in. × 4 in. × 8 ft. cedar
boards for the stiles (pine
also works if cedar is not
available, but rot-resistant
cedar is better for the stiles
if they'll be in contact with
wet soil or lawn)

One or two 3½-in. square
tapered bun feet (depending
on your design)

Large craft finial (optional)

Two 1 in. × 2 in. × 8 ft. pine
boards for the rails

1¼-in. no. 8 deck screws

Paint or stain (optional)

TOOLS

Compound miter saw with a
clamp attachment

Band saw or jigsaw

Sander

Awl (optional)

Drill/driver

Quick-flip drive with a #8
$^{11}/_{64}$-in. countersink bit

Clamps

Adjustable square

Drill bit that's smaller than
the shaft of the screw in the
craft finial

Since the screws are on the inside of the obelisk, and it's meant to be seen from far away (and possibly covered with vines), I chose not to counterbore screws and plug the screw holes. Instead, I countersunk the screw holes: predrilled only up to the triangular tip of the drill bit so the screw lies flush with the face of the wood.

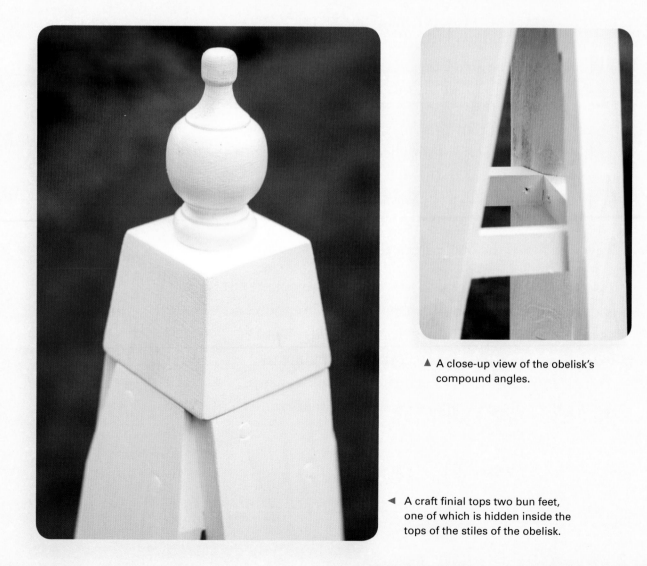

▲ A close-up view of the obelisk's compound angles.

◀ A craft finial tops two bun feet, one of which is hidden inside the tops of the stiles of the obelisk.

Making the Pyramid Shape

To form the pyramid shape, I used a 3½-in. square tapered bun foot, which I found in a hardware store (near other furniture feet and legs). If your hardware store doesn't carry them, cut a block of wood at 3⅝ in. square, center a 2¾-in. square at one end and cut the sides so that they taper toward the 2¾-in. square at the top. One end will be a 3⅝-in. square, the opposite end will be a 2¾-in. square, and the four sides will be trapezoids.

Cut the stiles. 1

From the 1 × 4 cedar boards, cut four stiles to the same length, about 4 ft.

Position the narrow end of the bun foot so that it's flush with one end of one of the stiles.

1 **Cut the stiles.** (Continued)

Trace the bun foot's two angled edges onto the stile.

Using a band saw or jigsaw, cut the two lines to give the stile a tapered end. If the cuts are wavy, smooth them out with a sander.

Trace the tapered end of the stile onto another stile and cut along the lines to make a second tapered stile. You'll have two stiles with tapered ends and two stiles without.

Attach the craft finial. (Optional) 2

If you're not using a second bun foot on top of the first, attach the craft finial now. Find the center of the small, tapered end of the bun foot by drawing an X from corner to corner. Use an awl to make a hole at the center of the X, or use the drill/driver to predrill a small hole (don't countersink this hole).

Screw the craft finial in place.

If you'd like the craft finial to rest on top of a second bun foot, as seen in the outdoor photos of this project, set this bun foot and craft finial assembly aside and use the second bun foot in step 3. If you don't want to use a second bun foot, use this bun foot and craft finial assembly in step 3.

Attach the stiles to the bun foot. 3

Predrill two holes at the top of each of the four stiles, with each hole positioned about ¾ in. from the corners where the bun foot will be attached, as shown.

(An alternative method is to trace the trapezoidal side of the bun foot on the tapered end of the stile, draw a line from one opposing corner to the other, and drill two holes along the line.)

OBELISK

243

3 Attach the stiles to the bun foot. (Continued)

Screw one of the tapered stiles to the finial, propping up the other end of the stile with a piece of scrap wood or a clamp fastened to the work surface.

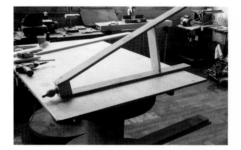

Screw the other tapered stile to the opposite side of the bun foot, using a piece of scrap as a support between the two stiles.

Center the remaining, square-ended pieces on the remaining bun foot faces and screw in place.

To prop up the last piece, I used the handle of a clamp.

Your obelisk has taken shape!

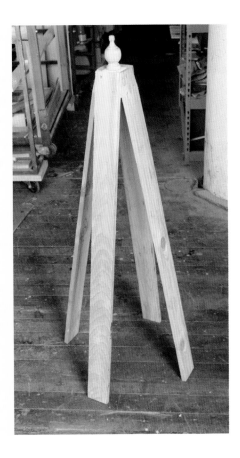

Cut the lower rails to approximate length. **4**

Cut the 1 × 2 pine boards into four lengths, each about 12 in. long.

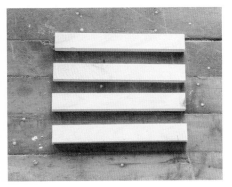

5 Set the angles of the compound miter saw and cut the lower rails. First you'll cut 5 degrees in one direction, and 45 degrees in the other direction.

Unplug the compound miter saw and set the tilt of its blade at 5 degrees.

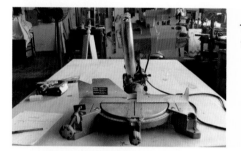

The blade should be tilted slightly to the left.

Set the angle of the table to 45 degrees by pressing the thumb button and pushing the knob on the front of the saw to the right, until the indicator says 45 degrees. Plug the saw back in.

Draw an arrow pointing up on the face of one of the rails. Stand the rail on its edge, so the face that doesn't have the arrow is against the fence.

Cut the end off this piece, starting from the corner.

Using an adjustable square, make a mark 11 in. from the outermost corner of the angled cut.

Place the board back on the saw, this time on the other side of the blade, with the arrow facing up.

Next, flip the board over so that the face with the arrow is against the fence with the arrow facing down.

5

Set the angles of the compound miter saw and cut the lower rails.
(Continued)

Cut along the mark you made at the 11-in. point. The piece should be 11 in. from the two outermost points of the trapezoid.

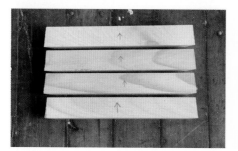

Repeat the steps above with the remaining three lower rails.

 6

Predrill holes and attach the lower rails to the obelisk.

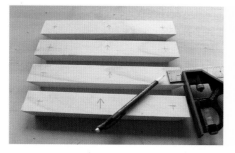

Use an adjustable square to center a mark 1 in. in from both ends of each of the lower rails.

Predrill at about a 45-degree angle as shown.

Center a mark on the insides of each stile 9¼ in. up from the bottom. Place one rail between two stiles with its outermost corners on the marks. The arrow will be on the inside face, facing up toward the peak of the obelisk. Screw in place.

Place another rail between the two opposite stiles and screw in place.

Screw the third and fourth lower rails in place.

6 **Predrill holes and attach the lower rails to the obelisk.** (Continued)

The lower rails are now in place.

7 **Cut and attach the middle rails.**

Use an adjustable square to center a mark on each stile 9¼ in. up from the top of the lower rails.

In the same manner as the other rails, cut four middle rails, with the distance between their outermost points measuring 8½ in.

Predrill two holes into each rail at 45 degrees.

Align the outermost points with the marks you've made on the stiles and screw the rails into place.

8 Cut and attach the upper rails. The upper rails are short boards, so when you're cutting them keep your hands away from the blade and use a miter saw clamp if you have one.

Center a mark on each stile 9¼ in. up from the top of the middle rails. In the same manner as the other rails, cut four upper rails, with the distance between their outermost points measuring 6 in.

Unlike the steps for the lower and middle rails, predrill the holes for the upper rails while each rail is placed on its marks to ensure the drill will fit between the stiles (the drill might not be going straight up—this is okay).

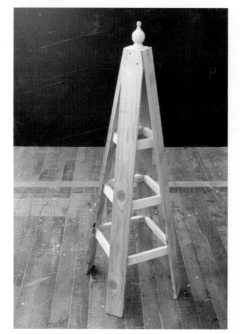

Screw all four upper rails in place.

9 If you're using a second bun foot, attach the bun foot and finial to the top of the obelisk. Paint or stain.

Acknowledgments

Ellen Blackmar for her unbelievable photos of the finished projects.

All those who helped Ellen and me make the photographs happen: Tam Lyn for her photography assistance; Linda Jackson, Paula Vining, Mary Bliss, and Allison Brown and Steven White for the use of their lovely gardens to photograph the finished pieces in; and Marina White for her knot-tying skills in the garden swing project and the lovely scones in the finished-piece photograph of the slat bench.

Tatsuki Katakura for painting and staining many of the projects in this book, and for his help sorting the hundreds of photos for this book.

The people who helped me launch my woodworking career, including Anne Conolly of Camp Onaway for Girls and Elaine Hamel of Girls At Work, Inc. who encouraged and empowered me to start teaching woodworking; Glenn Leonard and Greg Larson of the New England School of Architectural Woodworking who taught me cabinetmaking; and Lilah Crews-Pless, my partner in custom furniture making when we were both embarking on our careers.

The people at Timber Press, especially Juree Sondker, who fished my work out of the depths of the Internet and placed a perfectly timed phone call, to which I responded, "Yes! I will write a book!" Lesley Bruynesteyn combed through the text line by line to help make this into a book.

My friends who supported me during the process of making this book, including the good people at the New England Society of Information and Technology, where I built the projects, and my friends who gave solicited advice over the Internet on project design and paint color.

Linda Jackson, Fred Jackson, Laura Ware, and especially Joe DeMartino who helped edit my text and provided patience and endless support for my seemingly never-ending project.

◀ My nephew Patrick, who is just learning how to stand, checks out the view from above with the aid of a sturdy bench.

Metric Conversions

inches	centimeters
1/10	0.3
1/6	0.4
1/4	0.6
1/3	0.8
1/2	1.3
3/4	1.9
1	2.5
2	5.1
3	7.6
4	10
5	13
6	15
7	18
8	20
9	23
10	25

feet	meters
1	0.3
2	0.6
3	0.9
4	1.2
5	1.5
6	1.8
7	2.1
8	2.4
9	2.7
10	3

Further Reading

Books

The following are listed in ascending order of the reader's experience with woodworking.

Fraser, Aimé Ontario. *Getting Started in Woodworking: Skill-Building Projects That Teach the Basics.* Newtown, CT: The Taunton Press, 2003.

> A great book for beginners, full of skill-building sidebars and tips and tricks along the way as you build each of the five projects with well-written, in-depth instructions.

Walton, Stewart and Sally. *Painted Woodcraft: Projects & Techniques.* Great Britain: Ryland Peters & Small: 1997; New York: Sterling Publishing Co., 1997.

> A project-based book with photographs and illustrations of twenty-five simple and intermediate woodcraft projects and ten techniques for painted finishes.

Burton, Kenneth. *Cutting-Edge Band Saw Tips & Tricks.* Cincinnati, Ohio: Popular Woodworking Books, 2004.

> The band saw is my favorite woodworking machine because of its versatility and ease of use. This is the book I read when I was first getting acquainted with the band saws in my teaching woodshop: it provides an intimate understanding of maintenance, proper settings, and the amazing things a woodworker can do with this machine and a few other hand tools.

Hoadley, R. Bruce. *Understanding Wood: A Craftsman's Guide To Wood Technology.* Newtown, CT: The Taunton Press, 2000.

> This is the book for the woodworker who would like to gain a technical understanding of how trees grow, how timber is processed into lumber, how wood moves, and how to use this knowledge to create resilient, long-lasting wood projects.

Jackson, Albert; Day, David; Jennings, Simon. *The Complete Manual of Woodworking.* Great Britain: William Collins & Sons, 1989; 14th printing, New York: Alfred A. Knopf, 2014.

> An exhaustive reference to all things related to woodworking, including design, tools, planning a workshop, joinery, bending, veneering, carving, finishing, and fasteners, this book has beautiful, straightforward illustrations and photographs and well-organized information.

Websites

ana-white.com

Ana White creates woodworking projects
for all skill levels inspired by indoor and
outdoor furniture in popular stores such as
Pottery Barn, Restoration Hardware, and
Crate & Barrel.

instructables.com

Instructables has a huge range of projects
(and a huge range of quality) in every
category, often with detailed instruction
photographs, submitted by members of
the site.

Photography Credits

Photos on pages 2–50, 61, 62, 68, 75 (bottom), 76, 87, 88, 95, 96, 99–106, 112, 119, 120, 129 (bottom), 130, 138, 146, 154, 160–161, 162, 164, 176, 186, 193 (bottom), 194, 206–207, 208, 223, 224, 238, 240, 253, 254–255 by Ellen Blackmar.

All other photos by the author.

Index

© ELLEN BLACKMAR

Katie Jackson is a designer and builder of simple furniture using renewable and reclaimed materials. After graduating from Bennington College, where she studied painting and education, she trained as a cabinetmaker at New England School of Architectural Woodworking. In anticipation of leading the woodworking program at Camp Onaway for Girls, she attended a Woodworking Teacher's Education Program at Girls At Work, Inc., specializing in empowering at-risk girls with wood shop skills. Katie then headed the woodworking program at Camp Onaway for four summers, where many of the projects in this book were first built. Katie teamed up with Lilah Crews-Pless to launch a design-build collaboration out of TechShop San Francisco and TechShop Menlo Park, where they created flat-pack furniture from reclaimed materials.

Katie now builds at New England Society of Innovation and Technology (NESIT) Hackerspace, the wood shop photographed in this book. Other wood shops in which Katie has worked include Worthington Cabinetmakers and Champagne Tables; she's also built at makerspaces including TechShop San Francisco, TechShop Menlo Park, and Woodworkers' Club Norwalk. She has worked in the antiques business in Silicon Valley and has taught painting workshops at rePublicArt in New Haven, Connecticut. Katie lives with her boyfriend and her pit bull, Marmalade, in Connecticut. To see more of Katie's projects and to learn about her woodworking workshops, please visit katiejacksonwoodworks.com.

© TAM LYM

Ellen Blackmar is a professional photographer specializing in architectural, wedding, and portrait photography. She also creates personal work using large-format film and nineteenth-century-style cameras. She completed her undergraduate degree at Massachusetts College of Art and Design and has also attended programs at Rhode Island School of Design and The Center for Alternative Photography in New York. In her free time she enjoys cooking, horseback riding, and exploring the wilderness of her native New England. More of her work can be viewed at ellenrosephotography.com.